Buried Roots
and Indestructible
Seeds

T0163462

Buried Roots and Indestructible Seeds

The Survival of
American Indian Life
in Story, History, and Spirit

Edited by
Mark A. Lindquist
and Martin Zanger

The University of Wisconsin Press

The University of Wisconsin Press
114 North Murray Street
Madison, Wisconsin 53715

3 Henrietta Street
London WC2E 8LU, England

Copyright © 1993, 1994
The Board of Regents of the University of Wisconsin System
All rights reserved

5 4 3 2 1

Printed in the United States of America

Published with the cooperation of the
Wisconsin Humanities Council

Library of Congress Cataloging-in-Publication Data
Buried roots and indestructible seeds : the survival of American
   Indian life in story, history, and spirit / edited by Mark A.
Lindquist and Martin Zanger.
      168 p.   cm.
   Includes bibliographical references and index.
   ISBN 0-299-14440-2 (cl.).   ISBN 0-299-14444-5 (pb.)
   1. Indians of North America—History.   2. Indians of North
America—Folklore.   3. Indians of North America—
Social life and customs.   I. Lindquist, Mark Allan, 1952–
II. Zanger,   Martin.
E77.B95   1995
970.004′97—dc20   94-21162

Contents

Buried Roots
and Indestructible
Seeds

An Introduction

Kimberly M. Blaeser

University of Wisconsin–Milwaukee

I think you need a place to attach to in moments of fear and detachment and confusion, a place that's familiar, a dream place. I think it's an oral traditional place, which means that it's greater than reality and it's greater than a material place you would find on the earth. Gerald Vizenor, "Follow the Trickroutes"

The title for this collection, "Buried Roots and Indestructible Seeds," is taken from a central passage in Louise Erdrich's novel *Love Medicine.* In the novel, the protagonist Lipsha Morrisey has taken up a task his grandfather had done before him—digging dandelions. As he digs, he feels a lost power return to him and he thinks about the plant: "A buried root. A nuisance people dig up and throw in the sun to wither. A globe of frail seeds that's indestructible."[1] In the story of the novel, the dandelions come to symbolize the American Indians. Like the dandelions, Native Americans of this country have been seen as a nuisance cluttering up the landscape; like the "weeds," Indians of this country have been pulled up by their roots and expected to die; but, again like the globe of dandelion seeds, the tribal heritage, though frail, has proven itself indestructible, has endured and continually renewed itself. Thus the collection's subtitle: "The Survival of American Indian Life in Story, History, and Spirit."

The works in this volume, which grew out of a series of conferences sponsored by the Wisconsin Humanities Committee in 1990–1991, trace the struggle and indestructibility of Indian people in this country. Taken together, they give us some sense of just where that dandelion power, that survival power, of Indian people comes from.

In the quotation which opens this introduction, Gerald Vizenor speaks of the need to have a place, a dream place, an *oral traditional* place, that's greater than any physical reality. In the interview with Joseph Bruchac from which that comment is taken, Vizenor explains that this survival place cannot be on or of the earth because the earth will change. The historical essays in this collection by Frederick Hoxie, James Oberly, and Thomas Vennum, Jr., poignantly illustrate Vizenor's point; physical places have been lost to their original inhabitants in any number of ways. They have been flooded, taken in treaty negotiations, devastated by the lumber industry. Their natural features have been altered, their wildlife decimated. And yet, despite the loss of their homeland, despite the enforced changes to their lifestyle, Indian people have endured. Why? Where have they found the source of strength for that survival? In his interview with Bruchac, Vizenor says, "I see the permanence of things in a kind of oral traditional visual place."[2]

Is it possible, as Vizenor suggests, as several of the other essays in this collection suggest, that the oral traditions of a people could be so strong that they allow them to endure and survive all sorts of physical and emotional hardships, not only to endure but to continue the traditions? In speaking of his own tribe's tragic history and their survival, Kiowa writer N. Scott Momaday quotes Isak Dinesen: "All sorrows can be borne if you put them into story or tell a story about them." Momaday and Dinesen speak here of the discovery or "imagination of meaning," the use of storytelling to interpret events, to seek meaning in the chaos of life, or to create understanding of the happenings of history. So the very act of making a story, in its creation of meaning, is an act of survival. Thus, both the interpretations of experience and the creative stories of this volume not only trace the endurance of tribal people, but also contribute to their continuance.

But storytelling of indigenous peoples can be more than a way of understanding the past; it can teach a way of living that guarantees future survival. Joseph Bruchac, in the essay included here, speaks of the "circle of stories" which reveal to native people the relationships of all things. If we understand "the circularity of the world, how everything is connected and every action produces a result," we can understand our responsibility to the world. The traditional tales, then, such as those of Gluskabe which Bruchac tells, are more than entertainment. They can be seen as "ecological parables" which contain "the distilled wisdom of tens of thousands of years of experience." The "primary considerations" of the native tradition as passed on through the stories, says Bruchac, are "continuance and balance."

We need to look no further for proof of Bruchac's claim of the practical applicability of the stories than to the essays of Thomas Vennum, Jr., and George Cornell. In speaking of "Native American Perceptions of the Environment," Cornell underscores the same ecological ideas Bruchac has shown to be key in traditional stories: "universal interaction and purpose," and the " 'relatedness' of all beings in creation." The result of following these philosophies has been the maintenance of the fragile balance of the ecosystem as evidenced in such things as the "sustained yields" of wild rice Vennum describes, a balance accomplished through limited harvest and reseeding. The violation of these principles by the "conquerors" of North America, say both Cornell and Vennum, have brought about the extinction or near-extinction of many plant and animal species and have endangered our planet. For, in a linear tradition with a sense of an "unending frontier," explains Bruchac, it is easy "to forget what you leave behind." Several of the essays in the collection enumerate what has been left behind on Western civilization's journey to "conquer" nature: the great auk, the passenger pigeon, the heath hen, tens of thousands of rotting buffalo carcasses, the stumps of ancient redwood and cedar, a trail of herbicides and poisoned waterways. The tribal stories which teach co-existence and continuance rather than conquest and "use," are, Bruchac claims, "desperately needed by all Americans."

James Oberly's account of the Chippewa River Valley and Frederick Hoxie's account of treaty-making and treaty rights are likewise placed in the historical and philosophical context of conquest. The dam project which created the Chippewa Flowage altered the natural environment, flooded a tribal settlement, and threatened the subsistence economy of the Lac Courte Oreilles Ojibway—all in the interest of generating greater hydroelectric power for the march of civilization and all without tribal consent of the Indians themselves who said they "had rather have the reservation." In this flooding of more than eight thousand acres of the LCO reservation, the dam project also ran afoul of a United States treaty agreement. We see this Wisconsin event as but one of the stories of loss when Hoxie traces the broader history of the conquest of both the land and the tribes through the treaty process.

But Hoxie's account also ultimately attests to that dandelion power of the tribes who have themselves of recent years become involved in the legal battling for their treaty rights and have (in the "imagination of meaning") come to understand the treaties as "symbols of community allegiance," as documents which attest to their affliation with a certain tribe. "Ironically," writes Hoxie, Indian treaties which "were originally a badge of sovereignty for the national government," have become "badges of Native American sovereignty."

This turning of history and the twist of story in the interest of survival, leads us finally to the trickster essays of this volume (Blaeser's and Vizenor's) and to the short story by Denise Sweet. As Vizenor points out, the humor, irony, and liberation of the trickster stories of oral tradition offer a sustaining power that a tragic world view cannot. The tribal trickster figure fulfills various roles, but perhaps none more important than the embodiment of survival and what I call the "prerequisite to survival"—continuance. Come what may—flood, treaty, or an "educational experience" like that depicted in Sweet's short story—Trickster "just keeps going on," as does the sustaining storytelling tradition in Native American culture.

The survival humor of trickster and trickster story stems from and depends upon a communal experience. These stories emerge from the context of community and the comedy itself ultimately reforms that community. We can laugh together only because we inhabit a common understanding of the world, and our shared humor further cements our communal bonds. The imagination of Trickster in tribal stories not only helps to sustain native peoples but, Vizenor explains, simultaneously liberates them from circumstances and allows them to imagine themselves more richly.

And richly imagined is the world in the stories of Vizenor and Sweet, examples of the continuing storytelling tradition. Vizenor's excerpt from *The Heirs of Columbus* challenges and re-imagines the historical interpretation of Columbus, thus liberating us from the "invented Indian" identity created and perpetuated in the dominant historical and fictional accounts. Sweet's "Blackbird Women" embodies its own lesson of survival as it epitomizes the mettle of tribal character in the story's protagonist, illustrating clearly both the girl's fragility and her strength. We recognize that the child has power, dandelion staying power. But we see, too, how easily the institutions and the misplaced religious zeal of the Blackbird Women might tear apart the intricately woven globe of family, community, culture, and story that is the child's identity. Like the Indian people of history, the girl needs "any magic left" in her "just to stay alive." Her survival, like the historic survival of native peoples, like the survival of Indian people today, depends upon the strength of her connection to tradition.

Readers of this volume will no doubt discover that part of that enduring tradition has found its way into *Buried Roots and Indestructible Seeds.*

Notes

1. Louise Erdrich, *Love Medicine* (New York: Holt, Rinehart, and Winston, 1984), 215.

2. Gerald Vizenor, "Follow the Trickroutes," in *Survival This Way: Interviews with American Indian Poets* (Tucson: University of Arizona Press, 1987), 291.

Suggestions for Further Reading

Allen, Paula Gunn. *The Sacred Hoop: Recovering the Feminine in American Indian Traditions.* Boston: Beacon Press, 1986.

Bruchac, Joseph. *Survival This Way: Interviews with American Indian Poets.* Tucson: University of Arizona Press, 1987.

Campisi, Jack, and Laurence M. Hauptman, eds. *The Oneida Indian Experience: Two Perspectives.* Syracuse: Syracuse University Press, 1991.

Conn, Richard. *Circles of the World: Traditional Art of the Plains Indians.* Seattle: University of Washington Press, 1982.

de Usabel, Frances, and Jane A. Roeber, compilers. *American Indian Resource Manual for Public Libraries.* Madison: Division for Library Services, Wisconsin Department of Public Instruction, 1992.

Erdrich, Louise. *Love Medicine.* New York: Holt, Rinehart, and Winston, 1984. An expanded edition has been released by H. Holt (New York, 1993).

McNickle, D'Arcy. *Native American Tribalism: Indian Survivals and Renewals.* New York: Oxford University Press, 1973.

Matthiessen, Peter. *Indian Country.* New York: Viking Press, 1984.

Nabokov, Peter, ed. *Native American Testimony: A Chronicle of Indian and White Relations from Prophecy to the Present, 1492–1992.* New York: Viking Press, 1991.

Owens, Louis. *Other Destinies: Understanding the American Indian Novel.* Norman: University of Oklahoma Press, 1992.

Silko, Leslie Marmon. *Ceremony.* New York: Viking Press, 1977.

Turner, Frederick W., III ed. *The Portable North American Indian Reader.* New York: Viking Press, 1974.

Velie, Alan R., ed. *American Indian Literature: An Anthology.* Norman: University of Oklahoma Press; revised edition, 1991.

Welch, James. *Fools Crow.* New York: Viking Books, 1986.

The Circle of Stories

Joseph Bruchac, III

Waudjoset nudatlokugan bizwamigwi
alnoba bimisigeniganiye
agwedewabizun. Ta wawogit.

My story was out walking around, an old-time forest person with clothing of moss and ashwood withes for a belt. And here my story camps . . . my story of Gluskabe.

Long ago, when Tabaldak, the Creator, had finished making things, some of the dust remained on Tabaldak's hands. So Tabaldak brushed that dust off and as it fell down and sprinkled on the earth, the earth began to move and shape itself. Where that dust fell, the earth shaped itself into a body and then arms and hands and then a head. Then that earth which had shaped itself sat up and looked around.

Awani gia? Who are you? said Tabaldak.

Gluskabe nia. I am Gluskabe, said that earth which had shaped itself.

And so it was that Gluskabe came to be. That one whose name means "the one who speaks" or "the story teller," that one who was here before the human beings, that one named Gluskabe who came from the living earth.

9

The circle is one of the strongest shapes in nature. When we see the world from a Native American perspective, that circle shapes our vision. We find circles and the idea of the circle everywhere, from the shapes of most Native dwellings to the view of the world as a series of continual, repeating cycles. Human life, itself, is seen as a circle, as we come from our mother, the Earth, when we are born and return to that same earth when we die. It is commonly said among the Haudenausaunee people, the Iroquois, that the faces of our children who are yet to be born are just there, just under the surface of the earth. Death is not an ending, but a continuance of a natural cycle. Those who have died, those same Haudenausaunee people say, are no further from us than the other side of a fallen leaf. Although we are aware of the passage of the seasons and the years, there is a sense of stability and timelessness about this world. The world is larger than the human beings who dwell within its many cycles, who are part of its great circular design. Along with that recognition of the interrelationship of all things comes a sense of awe and gratitude towards the immense and wonderful creation which surrounds us. We find that expressed again and again in traditional Native stories, such as those my Abenaki ancestors told of Gluskabe.

All around Gluskabe was the Creation and he thought it was very beautiful. Then Gluskabe tried to sit up and walk around. But in his eagerness to see more he forgot that he had not yet shaped legs. He tried to push himself up, pushed hard to each side. The earth rose into two mountain ranges. Today they are called the Green Mountains of Vermont and the Adirondacks. But Gluskabe could not stand. Then he reached up to the top of those mountains to either side and tried to pull himself up. His fingers gouged down into the mountains, forming the channels or rivers. So Otter Creek and Little Otter Creek, the Lamoille and the Winooski and the other rivers which flow down were formed. But Gluskabe could not stand.

Then Gluskabe saw that Tabaldak was looking at him, looking

down at him. He looked where Tabaldak was looking and saw that he had forgotten, in his eagerness to stand, forgotten to shape legs for himself. Then he shaped legs for himself from the living earth and stood. Where he had been, there was now a great hole in the earth. The rivers filled it in with water and it became the great lake we called Bitonbowk, the "waters in between," Lake Champlain.

Then Gluskabe and Tabaldak wandered together. Everywhere they looked, they saw beauty. They climbed together to the mountaintop and gazed out, wide-eyed, at the beauty of creation all around them.

In those stories, we see the circularity of the world around us, how everything is connected and every action produces a result. In contrast, the Western world emphasizes straight lines, linear thinking and upward progress. Rather than continual return, the pattern in modern Western life is continual departure. Actions are taken with little or no thought for anything other than the immediate future. We go forward, leaving behind "childish things," we leave the place we were born, leave behind parents and grandparents, we advance in our careers by "moving upward" and being "upwardly mobile." This constant movement is socially and economically desirable. In this view of life, time becomes of utmost importance. "Time is money" in a capitalist society. Things are always changing and bound to the imposed rhythms of work days, offices, time clocks, overtime, saving time, taking time out. The ticking of the clock is more important than the beat of the human heart. And the spiritual dimensions of life, which were of such great importance to the ancestors of those Europeans who have constructed this worldview, dimensions once visible in great cathedrals and religious feasts, have become reduced to commercial symbols, empty shells of their former grandeur as the time clock replaces church time. At times, there seems to be little room for God in this modern world except as a surrogate for retail marketing—Christmas, for example, has perhaps its most powerful contemporary meaning as the time when people will buy more and help the consumer-based economy, rather than as the time to acknowledge the continued concern of a benevolent deity. The mechanization of human life is visible in factories where people are like replaceable parts—limited and expendable. Ironically, it is a world-view which sees human beings as being in control of nature, being "larger than life," at the same time that the individual is debased and spiritually disenfranchised.

Those two opposing world-views, one governed by the straight line, the other informed by the circle, first came into conflict with the arrival of Europeans in the western hemisphere approximately 500 years ago. They remain in opposition to this day. Despite the overwhelming technological military superiority of western cultures and the biological accident of the original natives of this hemisphere having no resistance to the innumerable new diseases brought by the Europeans, the Native world-view remains strong to this day. It has been preserved nowhere more strongly than in the traditional stories which are told by Native people, stories which point out the relationship between human beings and the natural world. These stories are so deeply based on a close observance for thousands of years of nature and the effect which human actions have upon the world that it is not an exaggeration to describe them as "ecological parables." Even though the word *ecology* (defined by *Webster's New Riverside Dictionary* as "the science of the interaction and relationships between living organisms and their environment") introduces a very new concept in Western thought, it is very ancient for the Native people of this hemisphere. But instead of calling it "ecology," they called it "life."

———————

Before I say more about traditional stories, about how they were used and continue to be used by Native people, let me say a few more things about those two symbols, the circle and the straight line, and what I see as the logical consequences of following each as a pattern of behavior.

Take any group of people, whether it be children or adults, and place them in a room arranged in the typical way rooms are arranged in places designed for learning—in classrooms or lecture halls. Such architecture, of course, relies upon straight lines. Each person is seated in a row and facing forward. The rows are unconnected to each other. Those in back cannot see the faces of those in front of them. Those furthest in front have no vision at all of those seated behind. And the only one you are supposed to see (keep your eyes front!) is the authority figure, the teacher at the head of the classroom, the one who knows everything.

Hierarchies and levels of power grow naturally out of such alignments. In fact, bend a straight line twice so that it connects back and you have a pyramid, not a circle. That was the shape of the political and spiritual universe as seen in Europe from the middle ages to the time of those first documented voyages of exploration to the New World. In the political pyramid, the king is at the top, the lords and nobles just below him, and the great mass of the people at the bottom, supporting it all, owning the least, and furthest from God. In the spiritual pyramid, the pope is at the top, the bishops and priests just below him, and the great mass of people at the bottom supporting it all, owning the least and furthest from God. When you are sitting in straight lines, or when you are part of a pyramid shaped of three straight lines, it matters very much where you sit and most people are going to be uncomfortable with where they are sitting.

If you take that same classroom and rearrange it, change it from rows of straight lines to a single circle, something begins to happen. For one, the individual's attention and their perception of their own place in the schemes of things changes. Now everyone is the same distance from the center, everyone can see everyone else's face, and everyone is seated at the same height. Everyone's voice carries much more equal weight in the circle. Everyone also has much more attention focussed upon them—it is harder to hide in a circle than in a series of rows where you can sit way in the back and keep a low profile. Therefore, you are more responsible and more a part of everything when you are part of a circle. What goes around will eventually come to you.

One more thing about that straight line. When you always move forward, it is easy to forget what you leave behind. If you spoil your environment and have a sense of an unending frontier, a better place beyond the next hill, then you may rationalize your irresponsibility as "progress" and "inevitable." (As Ronald Reagan used to say when he hosted the General Electric Theater on television in the late sixties: "Progress is our most important product.") Yet if one were ever able to truly travel in an unbending straight line, sooner or later their path will take their feet from the earth and their journey will carry them out of this world, away from the light and life of our planet.

In many ways, the Western view of the world—both the natural world around us and the intimate world of the human family— remains shaped by linear thinking, straight lines, and hierarchies. And just as a dominant male is usually seen as the "natural" head of the family (like the paternal God in Heaven), so, too, the human being (usually viewed as a male) is seen as being in charge of nature, controlling it, using it as humans see fit. If immediate financial profit can be made from it, then it is only logical in such a world view, to give one visible contemporary example, to support policies which lead directly to the clear-cutting of the ancient northwest coast forests of North America and the rain forests of South America, Africa, and Asia. The resultant loss of thousands of species, the degradation of the environment, the consequences for untold generations to come appear to be of secondary importance for those who make the decisions. Contrast that with the words of Chan K'in, a hundred-year old Mayan elder (quoted from *The Last Lords of Palenque* by Victor Perea and Robert D. Bruce). "The roots of all living things," he said, "are tied together. When a mighty tree is felled, a star falls from the sky; before you cut down a mahogany you should ask permission of the keeper of the forest, and you should ask permission of the keeper of the star."

In the circular view, no one person—male or female—and no one species takes precedence. We human beings are, in the Native view, members of a large extended family which includes not only human relatives, but also animals and birds and plants, and even the winds, the waters, and the stones. In that family, everything is alive and everything is deserving of respect. If that respect is not given, if things are done wrongly, then there will be unfortunate consequences. Thus, the decision to cut even a single tree, or to kill a single animal, is a decision that cannot be made quickly or taken lightly. Continuance and balance are the primary considerations, not human comfort, or material or financial gain. Systems based on this "circular logic" therefore tend to be self-sustaining and stable. This does not, however, mean such systems are stiff or static. The natural world is a dynamic state of continual change, and to seek balance and insure continuance in such a world—where such violent events as hurricanes, earthquakes, and volcanic eruptions are among the more dramatic examples of that dynamism—means that human beings must remain alert, observant, open to learn from what they experience, and ready to adapt. Such alertness, observation, understanding, and adaptability can also be found in Native stories. In fact, it might be argued that Western hierarchical systems and the shaping of policies based almost entirely on ideas of financial profit and loss are the systems which are most stiff, static, and unable to adapt to change. This may be exemplified by the increasingly rapid ecological degradation of the planet, such as the destruction of the ozone layer, resulting from policies driven by economic considerations.

———————

Long ago, the story goes, Gluskabe decided to go hunting. But all the animals hid from him. He was not happy. So he went home and asked his grandmother Woodchuck to make him a game bag. She made him one of deer hairs, but Gluskabe said it was not good enough. So, too, he did not accept the game bags she made of caribou and moose hairs.

"What kind of game bag do you want, Gluskabe?" Grandmother Woodchuck said.

"I want one made of woodchuck hairs."

So Grandmother Woodchuck plucked all the hair from her belly. To this day all woodchucks have no hair on their bellies because of what she did. She made a game bag which did not look as good as the others, but it was the best one of all. It was magical. No matter how much was put into it, it could hold more.

Gluskabe thanked his Grandmother. Then he went into the forest and began to moan and weep. "Ah," he moaned, "all the animals are going to perish."

The animals heard this and came to him. "What is wrong?" they asked.

"Ah," Gluskabe said, "the world is going to disappear and you will surely die for you will have no place to stand."

This frightened the animals and they asked Gluskabe what they could do. Then Gluskabe smiled. "I have an idea," he said, "you can hide in my game bag."

So the animals all crawled into his game bag, all of the animals in the world. Then Gluskabe tied the top and took it home. But when his grandmother saw him enter, she spoke to him.

"What do you have there, Gluskabe?" she said.

"A great thing, Grandmother," Gluskabe said. "Now we no longer have to work hard to catch game animals. We need only reach into my game bag and take out what we want."

Grandmother Woodchuck looked into the game bag and all the animals in the world looked up at her. "Gluskabe," she said, "this will not do. One person cannot own all the game animals. And in this game bag, they will surely sicken and die. What will our children and our children's children do without game animals? And it is right that we must work to catch them. That way we grow stronger and the game animals too grow stronger seeking to escape us.

Gluskabe understood. He went back into the forest and opened his game bag. "Come out," he said to the animals. "The world disappeared, but I made it come back."

Then the game animals crawled out and went back into the forest. They are there to this day.

The Native world-view, which is expressed in traditional "folk stories, myths and legends" (which I prefer to refer to simply as "traditions"), was not shaped quickly on the continents of North and South America. The lessons carried by traditional tales are the result of tens of thousands of years of alertness, observation, understanding and adaptation. If a story tells of the bad consequences of the wanton destruction of game animals, that story is not a mere philosophical abstraction, but a result of experience. Moreover, those stories and other traditions often contain specific knowledge which can be of benefit. Traditions of folk medicine, for example, often backed up by stories, have proven to be the source of innumerable remedies now being used by the Western world as a whole. It is now widely accepted that there are thousands of plants to be found in the rain forests of the world which are known as medicine plants to Native people, but remain unknown to "modern science." Ironically, many—if not all—of those medicine plants are threatened with extinction. I recall a conversation I had once with Louis Oliver, a Creek elder from Oklahoma who became known in his seventies as a poet and fiction writer. "When you gather herbs," Louis said, "you never take the first one you see. Wait till you find you a bunch of them and then only take what you need. And before you go, loosen the earth and plant the seeds from the ones you take. Then say thank you." Showing respect for the plants, which provide us with remedies, is not superstition, but common sense.

———————

Respect for everything is a central concept taught by the stories. Within the family, that same respect was to be shown not only to adults but to children. In fact, the uses of stories in instruction exemplify the attitude of treating children with respect. Native people regarded it as wrong to beat children—and that attitude is still very common in Native communities to this day. Instead of striking a child who did wrong, telling a lesson story would be a first step towards correcting the child's behavior, because a story can show the results of inappropriate actions such as disrespect for elders, wasting food, bullying, and boasting. Striking a child could produce a number of bad results. For one, it might break a child's spirit and that child would not grow up straight and strong. For another, the child usually remembers the beating much more than whatever lesson it was supposed to teach—whereas a story goes deep into a person and remains there. Third, it is not brave for a big person to strike a small one—that is a bad example for children. Might does not make right and innumerable tales of smaller, weaker creatures outwitting those who are huge and powerful can be found in every Native tradition. Lastly—and having two grown sons who are much bigger and stronger than I am makes me very fond of this point— what will happen to you when the day comes when your children are big and strong and you are small and weak? It is dangerous to recycle violence. Respect that what you give today will return to you tomorrow.

One last point must be made. We live in a world of stereotyping, and it seems as if Native people are either being presented as one stereotype or another—either as brutish ignorant savages or as wise, all-knowing spiritual caretakers. I do not believe that Native American people are wiser than any other group in America. They are human beings like everyone else. However, their stories are, I firmly believe, the wisest and most useful body of knowledge to be found on this continent. Those stories contain the distilled wisdom of tens of thousands of years of experience. It is because Native Americans are as capable of wrong action and foolish errors as any human beings anywhere in the world that we need these lesson stories, we need to stay close to the circle. Lesson stories keep the Native people of each generation from repeating errors which their ancestors made. And today, because (as Sitting Bull is reputed to have said) "there are no longer just Indians here," that circle of stories is desperately needed by all Americans.

Round House

Whether Earth lodge
or seat lodge,
wigwam or wickiup
or tipi where
the sweet water sound
of the peyote drum
may be heard
the buildings
of Indian people
were round.

The floor of the house
stood for this Earth
on which we all live,
Mother of us all.

Walls stood for Sky
which arches above,
grants us the rain,
holds warm light
which brings life.

Its roundness was that
of the sacred circle
no beginning or end
and no corners like those
in a white man's house.

Some old people say
they have never learned
to like living in houses
with such sharp corners
where sacred things
like peace pipes and children
always seem to get lost.

(from *Translator's Son* by Joseph Bruchac)

JOSEPH BRUCHAC, III, is an editor, poet, storyteller, and teacher. He has authored four non-fiction books, three books of fiction, seven books of folk stories, sixteen books of poetry, and has edited eleven anthologies. His poetry has appeared in many magazines, and his *Breaking Silence* won the National Book Award in 1984. He holds a B.A. in English from Cornell University and a Ph.D. in comparative literature from Union Graduate School. Bruchac is the director of the *Greenfield Review* Literary Center in Greenfield Center, New York.

Suggestions for Further Readings

Benton-Benai, Edward. *The Mishomis Book: The Voice of the Ojibway.* St. Paul, MN: Red School House, 1988.

Bruchac, Joseph. *Dawn Land.* Golden, CO: Fulcrum Press, 1993.

Bruchac, Joseph, ed. *Songs from the Earth on Turtle's Back: Contemporary American Indian Poetry.* Greenfield Center, N.Y.: Greenfield Review, 1983.

Bruchac. Joseph. *Translator's Son.* Merrick, NY: Cross-Cultural Communications, 1980.

Bruchac, Joseph, and Michael Caduto. *Keepers of the Earth: Native American Stories and Environmental Activities.* Golden, CO: Fulcrum Press, 1988.

Crosby, Alfred W., Jr. *The Columbian Exchange: Biological and Cultural Consequences of 1492.* Westport, CT: Greenwood Press, 1972.

Crosby, Alfred W., Jr. *Ecological Imperialism: The Biological Expansion of Europe, 900–1900.* New York: Cambridge University Press, 1986.

Dobyns, Henry F. *Native American Historical Demography: A Critical Bibliography.* Bloomington: Indiana University Press, 1976.

Erdoes, Richard, and Alfonzo Ortiz, eds. *American Indian Myths and Legends.* New York: Pantheon Books, 1985.

Martin, Calvin, ed. *The American Indian and the Problem of History.* New York: Oxford University Press, 1987.

Morey, Sylvester M., and Olivia Gilliam, eds. *Respect for Life: The Traditional Upbringing of American Indian Children.* New York: Myrin Institute Books, 1974.

Nabokov, Peter and Robert Easter. *Native American Architecture.* New York: Oxford University Press, 1989.

Ruoff, A. Lavonne Brown. *American Indian Literatures: An Introduction, Bibliographic Review, and Selected Bibliography.* Modern Language Association, 1990.

Walters, Anna Lee, Peggy Beck, and Nia Francisco, eds. *The Sacred: Ways of Knowledge, Sources of Life.* Tsaile, AZ: Navajo Community College Press, 1977.

Wolf, Eric R. *Europe and the People without History.* Berkeley: University of California Press, 1982.

Native American Perceptions of the Environment

George L. Cornell

Michigan State University

T he term Native American refers to an enormously diverse population that resided on the North American continent for thousands of years before contact with Europeans. There were well over two thousand culturally distinct and autonomous groups of indigenous peoples inhabiting North America in the pre-Columbian era[1] This is well substantiated by the fact that these groups of people spoke over 550 different languages[2] and exhibited cultural diversity in subsistence patterns, ecological adaptations, housing patterns, kinship systems and many other areas. Collectively, Europeans would refer to these diverse peoples as "Indians." This infamous misnomer has confounded Native peoples over the centuries. Many of the New England nations, or tribes, during the early contact period would express dismay over being called "Indians." They eventually realized that the term referred to all Native inhabitants of the region, that it was an outgroup name, an imposed name used to describe the collectivity of non-European peoples.[3]

The term "Indian" or "Native American" does not include concepts of sovereignty and diversity. Each group of indigenous people had a name for referring to themselves. The Anishnabeg, the Ikce Wicasa, and the Odawa would become known in the post-contact historical period as the Chippewa, the Sioux, and the Ottawa. These individual names would be further corrupted and negated by the common usage of the term "Indian" to describe all Native peoples.

Like the diversity that was exhibited in group names, indigenous peoples have differing perceptions of the environment and the natural order of the universe, but there are also similarities among these spiritual ideologies. All indigenous peoples have a cosmological interpretation of the creation of the world, and many themes in Native American philosophy/spirituality tend to recur among differing groups. The prominent role of twins, often representing the polarities of human nature, the trickster as cultural hero, and the significance of the number four, which represents yearly cycles and the directions of the universe, are commonly shared by many Native peoples.

Generalizations about Native American philosophy/spirituality are also on firm footing when discussing the earth. Native peoples almost universally view the earth as a feminine figure. The Mother provides for the sustenance and well-being of her children: it is from her that all subsistence is drawn. The relationship of Native peoples to the earth, their Mother, is a sacred bond with the creation.

The masculine counterpart to the earth mother is the sky father. Native peoples regard the heavens as the domain of the Creator, or the Great Mystery, as this force has been described. The sun in particular often personifies masculine power. The relationship between the earth mother and sky father is perceived as a continuous love affair, in which Native peoples are allowed to witness and participate. The power of the sun and the rains that impregnate the earth mother provide the necessities of life for Native peoples. These products of love are sacred, and are to be respected and treated with great care. All behaviors of Native peoples, in some way, are related to this perception of universal interaction and purpose.

Native peoples viewed many of the products of the natural environment as gifts from the Creator. This was particularly true of their relationship to animals. Adrian Tanner in *Bringing Home Animals* clearly states this relationship. "Men make gifts to the animal world, that is, to the bush, and in return are the recipients of gifts of game animals killed by the hunters."[4] Man, in the Native American conception of the world, was not created to "lord" over other beings, but rather to cooperate and share the bounty of the earth with the other elements of the creation. All things in this creation had an essence, a reason for being, and this relationship was taken very seriously. Man was to function as a caretaker of the environment. Animals, air, water, and plants all coexisted in a fragile harmony that needed to be maintained to ensure the continuation of the people. This notion of continuity manifests itself in the Native American adherence to the circle or cycle of life.

Christopher Vecsey and Robert W. Venables address the concept of the "sacred circle" in the introduction to their text, *American Indian Environments: Ecological Issues in Native American History*, as follows:

The American Indians' concept of the sacred circle expresses a physical and spiritual unity. This circle of life is interpreted according to the particular beliefs of each Indian nation but is broadly symbolic of an encompassing creation. The English verb "environ" has as its first definition in the *Oxford English Dictionary:* "Of things: To form a ring around, surround, encircle." While non-Indians quite willingly admit to the complexity of the circle of "things" around them, what has been left behind by the scientific, post-Renaissance non-Indian world is the universal sacredness—the living mystery—of creation's circle. One of the themes of this book is the consequence of a conflict during which most indigenous Indian nations, who saw their environments as the sacred interdependence of the Creator's will, confronted waves of post-Renaissance Europeans who saw in the environment a natural response ordained by God for their sole benefit.[5]

This statement, which provides accurate insight into the environmental perceptions of Native peoples, emphasizes the "relatedness" of all beings in the creation. Unfortunately, many people refuse to acknowledge the credibility of such "obvious" statements about the nature of Native American views. The simplicity of the contentions which are at the heart of Native American philosophy often elude scholars. As an example, William A. Starna, in his review of *American Indian Environments*, condemned the notion of a sacred circle as "pan-Indian mythology."[6] The insensitivity inherent in this statement is confirmed by the reviewer's lack of understanding of the concluding chapter in Vecsey and Venables's text. The final chapter is entitled "An Iroquois Perspective" and is authored by Oren Lyons.

In his review, Starna refers to Lyons's essay as "a very brief but rambling account"[7] and casts doubts about the intended meaning and message of Lyons's essay. Starna does not perceive the implicit reality for Native peoples, particularly the Iroquois, of the existence of a "sacred circle." Lyons seems to address the issue:

> Respect the proper manner so that the seventh generation will have a place to live in. Let us look at the large issues. We are concerned with all the children of this earth. We are concerned with the four colors of man. Natural Law is very simple. You cannot change it; it prevails over all. There is not a tight rule, there is no court, there is not a group of nations in this world that can change this Natural Law. The Indians understood this Natural Law. They built their laws to coincide with Natural Laws. And that's how we survived.[8]

Lyons refers to what can be called the "sacred circle." The existence of "Natural Laws" is a contemporary reality for a prominent leader of the Onondaga Nation, and this present manifestation has strong historical roots among many Native American groups.

In 1854, Chief Seattle of the Swamish and Suquamish Tribes issued a statement in response to a federal request to purchase the lands of the northwest from the Native peoples who traditionally lived there. His response sheds a great deal of light on the concepts that have been presented here, and for this reason it will be quoted at length.

> Yonder sky that has wept tears of compassion upon our fathers for centuries untold, and which to us looks eternal, may change. Today it is fair, tomorrow it may be overcast with clouds.

> My words are like the stars that never set. What Seattle says the Great Chief at Washington can rely upon with as much certainty as our paleface brothers can rely upon the return of the seasons.

> The son of the Great Chief says his father sends us greetings of friendship and good will. This is kind of him, for we know he has little need of our friendship in return because his people are many. They are like the grass that covers the vast prairies, while my people are few; they resemble the scattering trees of a storm-swept plain.

> My people are ebbing away like a fast-receding tide that will never flow again. The White man's God cannot love his red children or He would protect them. We seem to be orphans who can look nowhere for help.

> How, then, can we become brothers? How can your God become our God and renew our prosperity and awaken in us dreams of returning greatness?

> Your God seems to be partial. He came to the white man. We never saw Him, never heard His voice. He gave the white man laws, but had not word for his red children whose teeming millions once filled this vast continent as the stars fill the firmament.

> No. We are two distinct races, and must ever remain so, with separate origins and separate destinies. There is little in common between us.

> To us the ashes of our ancestors are sacred and their final resting place is hallowed ground, while you wander far from the graves of your ancestors and, seemingly, without regret.

Your religion was written on tablets of stone by the iron finger of an angry God, lest you might forget it. The Red Man could never comprehend nor remember it.

Every part of this country is sacred to my people. Every hillside, every valley, every plain and grove has been hallowed by some fond memory or some sad experience of my tribe. Even the rocks, which seem to lie dumb as they swelter in the sun along the silent sea shore in solemn grandeur thrill with memories of past events connected with the lives of my people.

The very dust under your feet responds more lovingly to our foot-steps than to yours, because it is the ashes of our ancestors, and our bare feet are conscious of the sympathetic touch, for the soil is rich with the life of our kindred.

The white man will never be alone. Let him be just and deal kindly with my people, for the dead are not powerless.

Dead—did I say? There is no death. Only a change of worlds![9]

There is a great deal of controversy about the authenticity of the quotes which are attributed to Chief Seattle, and I would like to clarify this and provide support for the version which has been cited here. There is no doubt that enormous license has been taken with the words of Seattle. As an example, read the version of the Point Elliott Treaty speech which has been copyrighted and circulated by the Augsburg Publishing Company of Minneapolis, Minnesota.[10] The distortion clouds the intended meaning of the Sachem's speech, and the corruption of language seems to be aimed at promoting brotherhood, which, as illustrated by the above quote, was not the result that Seattle sought. The version of Seattle's speech which is cited above appeared in the *Seattle Sunday Star* on October 29, 1887. It was recorded by Dr. Henry A. Smith, who had been present at the Point Elliott negotiations. The authenticity of the quote has been attested to by Vivian M. Carkeek, who had discussed the matter with Smith before he died. A Seattle attorney, Clark R. Belknap, supports the authenticity of the transcription as it appears in *Chief Seattle's Unanswered Challenge*, and his conversation with Carkeek was witnessed by William A. Harris, an associate of Carkeek.[11]

Chief Seattle was not speaking in metaphoric language when he referred to the land as sacred. The elements of creation were kindred, and to be respected in perpetuity. Throughout the recorded history of Indian-White relations there have been numerous statements by indigenous peoples that verify the attitudes and perceptions of Seattle. The Lakota (Sioux) holyman Black Elk would lament that the "Nation's hoop" was broken when the unrelated culture of the non-Indian took possession of the lands of the Seven Fires. The classic *Black Elk Speaks*, an account of the life of Black Elk as told to John Neihardt, presents an insightful description of Lakota philosophy, which points out the "inter-relatedness" of man to the natural environment. Again, the concept of the circle, this time being characterized as a "hoop."[12]

J.R. Walker's *The Sun Dance and Other Ceremonies of the Oglala Division of the Teton Sioux* contains one of the most descriptive "sacred circle" narratives, obtained from an informant named Tyon prior to 1917.

> The Oglala believe the circle to be sacred because the Great Spirit caused everything in nature to be round except stone. Stone is the implementation of destruction. The sun and sky, the earth and moon are round like ths shield, though the sky is deep like a bowl. Everything that breathes is round like the body of man. Everything that grows from the ground is round like the stem of a tree. Since the Great Spirit has caused everything to be round, mankind should look upon the circle as sacred for it is the symbol of all things in nature except stone. It is also the symbol of the circle that marks the edge of the world and therefore the four winds that travel there. Consequently, it is also the symbol of a year. The day, the night, and the moon go in a circle above the sky. Therefore the circle is a symbol of these divisions of time and hence the symbol of all time.[13]

The idea of the planets' cyclic motion, as well as their physical shape, and direct observation of nature have reinforced the sacredness of the circle. There is a continuity present in the Native American conception of the environment throughout the post-contact period which is very strong and easily recognized. In *Seeing With A Native Eye: Essays on Native American Religion*, Barre Toelken argues that there is a continuity of cultural perceptions of the physical environment among the Pueblos.

> We might consider the Pueblo view that in the springtime Mother Earth is pregnant, and one does not mistreat her anymore than one might mistreat a pregnant woman. When our technologists go and try to get Pueblo farmers to use steel plows in spring, they are usually rebuffed. For us it is a technical idea—"Why don't you just use the plows? You plow, and you get 'X' results from doing so." For the Pueblos this is meddling with the formal religious idea (in Edward Hall's terms). Using a plow, to borrow the Navajo phrase, "Doesn't hold any sheep." In other words, it does not make any sense in the way in which the world operates. It is against the way things really go. Some Pueblo folks still take the heels off their shoes, and sometimes the shoes off their horses, during the spring. I once asked a Hopi whom I met in the country, "Do you mean to say, then, that if I kick the ground with my foot, it will botch everything up, so nothing will grow?" He said, "Well, I don't know whether that would happen or not, but it would just really show what kind of a person you are."[14]

Oren Lyons, Chief Seattle, Tyon, Black Elk, and the unidentified Hopi all address Native American perceptions of the environment and the human relationship to it. These environmental perceptions—which were in practice the attitudes, values, and beliefs of Native peoples as they interacted with the land, flora and fauna, and other intangible forms of existence (spirits)—formed the core of Native American adaptations to the natural world. Environmental perceptions of Native Americans were responsible for dictating behaviors and defining the limits of Man-Nature relations. The above statements emphasize the need for individual respect and a spiritual tie to the natural world. The "sacred hoop," or cycle of life, is not something to be tampered with. These diverse examples of Native American images of the earth provide a fore-glimpse of what would become touted as the twentieth-century outdoor ethic.

These elements of Native American philosophy became very appealing to segments of the American population at the close of the nineteenth century. The appeal stemmed from the radical changes that took place in American society. Large urban areas came into existence as a result of the enormous number of immigrants who came to the United States seeking employment opportunities or escaping from European conflicts. This influx of people caused a noticeable decline in the quality of life for most working-class people in the urban areas. This, when coupled with the "passing of the great west," produced a cultural milieu that was unrelated to the land and natural environment. This "unrelatedness" was noticed by diverse observers of American society. Black Elk noticed it, as did the American poet and author William Carlos Williams, who vividly wrote about it in his collection of essays *In the American Grain*, where he described the contemporary American as, "an Indian robbed of world."[15] The impact of the Industrial Revolution upon the environment and the "settlement" of the West, along with the destruction of its wildlife, ushered in the age of environmental thought.

The American West harbored tremendous herds of American bison in the mid-twentieth century, but during the decades of 1870–89, hide hunters who flooded the West decimated them. Not until 1871 did a viable bison hide market develop. Prior to this time, hides were left to rot on the plains, while meat was sold to railroads, army posts, or to local restaurants for table fare. Buffalo hides were not desired prior to 1871 because they were difficult to tan. Many of the early tanning experiments with buffalo hides were conducted in England and Germany. When these efforts proved unsuccessful, the market for hides as lap robes or leather products rapidly escalated. By 1883, most of the great herds of American bison had been exhausted. Much of the depredation of the buffalo was the result of local citizenry who sought get-rich-quick schemes. They perceived the bison slaughter as a way to supplement local wages and provide needed meat.[16]

The demise of the buffalo was also tied to the control and domination of western Native American populations. Although primarily caused by economic motivations, the destruction of the bison was welcomed by the United States Army as a military solution to the "Indian problem." If Native Americans did not have access to the continued food supply provided by the buffalo, they would have to become dependent on the federal government. Frank Mayer, one of the most notorious hide hunters, commented upon the ease of acquiring ammunition from the military to kill buffalo.[17] The policy of encouraging the destruction of the buffalo lured large numbers of hunters to pursue the "shaggies."

The destruction of the American bison marks the zenith of exploitative practices and thoughts in the late nineteenth century. Decimation of the buffalo had the effect of freeing up major range areas that would be consolidated into large ranches that were already flourishing in some areas of the West. The buffalo, a free grazer, would be supplanted by the steer, an animal which could be corralled, controlled, and genetically manipulated to produce saleable beef. This contrast between the bison and the steer provides insight into the nature of non-Indian environmental perceptions in the late nineteenth century.

At the close of the nineteenth century, the contemporary non-Indian perception of the environment emphasized the necessity of bringing the natural world under the control of "man." The earth was to be dominated and used to provide not only human basic needs, but a margin of profitability. This process of utilization was not accompanied by a philosophy which "related" humans to the environment. The concepts of surplus and markets were closely allied with the contemporary perceptions of resources, and these perceptions dictated behaviors toward the natural world. Under the auspices of Social Darwinism, American business demanded that only the strong survive. A philosophy of exploitation, which led to the extermination of the great auk, the passenger pigeon, and the heath hen, among others, permeated the American psyche. Most Americans perceived animals as mere commodities, not as fellow beings, and this perception quickened the pace of competition for animal resources and exacerbated environmental depredation. The American bison has come to symbolize this epoch in American history. Cy Martin described the role of the bison in the American West.

> The buffalo played an important part in the opening of the West. Without him, railroads would have gone bankrupt, homesteaders would have starved, and perhaps Indians would still roam the Great Plains of our western states. The buffalo, with his shaggy hair and hump, is a symbol of the growth of the United States. We, like the Indians, should consider him with awe and respect.[18]

This statement is an ironic eulogy for the American bison, already gone.

The focusing of public attention upon the exploitation of animal resources in the United States signaled the advent of conservationist thought, which would eventually develop into the contemporary "outdoor ethic." This development was not without ironic twists, for while the Congress was protecting Yellowstone Park in 1872, it was also condoning the destruction of the American bison via military appropriations that allowed hide hunters to obtain free powder and lead from army installations. Conservationist thought would develop very slowly between 1870 and 1900, but it would accelerate as the rapacious destruction of animal resources continued. The need for an ethical relationship between man and the environment would become a common-sensical adaptation to the demise of game populations. The development of this ethical tie with the environment would be significantly influenced by the examples and philosophy of Native Americans as the destruction of wild game became more prevalent.

It must be stated, though, that Native Americans did play a role in the decline of natural resources on the North American continent. Native peoples benefitted from and participated in the destruction of animal populations, particularly the beaver and large western hooved mammals, during the contact period. However, when

Indians did take part in the destruction of game animals during the historic contact period and into the late nineteenth century, it was not for the same reasons that non-Indian market hunters did. Subsistence and cultural autonomy were prime motivators for Native American participation in the trade.

The role of Native Americans in the destruction of game animals has been addressed by Calvin Martin's *Keepers of the Game: Indian-Animal Relationships and the Fur Trade*. This text has generated a great deal of critical interest, and it is important to any discussion of Native peoples as conservationists. Martin postulates that Native Americans, who were engaged in the fur trade, waged a war of "revenge" against furbearers, in particular the beaver. He surmises that the effects of European diseases, which decimated Native populations, were eventually attributed to the beaver, and this provided the rationale for Native hunters to exploit the beaver for the fur trade.

The work is a provocative attempt to provide a new rationale for the behavior of Native hunters in the fur trade, but Martin's contentions are weakly supported, and the argument is riddled with contradictions. He contends that the image of Native Americans as conservationists is simply a popular stereotype.

Late in the 1960's the North American Indian acquired yet another stereotypic image in the popular mind: the erstwhile "savage," the "drunken" Indian, the "vanishing" Indian was conferred the title of the "ecological" (i.e., conservationist-minded) Indian. Propped up for everything that was environmentally sound, the Indian was introduced to the American public as the great high priest of the Ecology Cult. Depending upon's one point of reference, this might appear to be another crass commercial gimmick, a serious case of misread or ignored history, or a logical outgrowth of the conservation movement. Actually it was some of all three. The idea would never have taken hold had it not been that the conservationists needed a spiritual leader at that particular point in time, and the Indian, given the contemporary fervor and theology of environmentalism, seemed the logical choice.[19]

Martin's perception of Native peoples as non-conservationists, when coupled with his allegation that Native Americans engaged in a war of revenge on the beaver, portrays Native peoples as exploiters and disavows the consistently reiterated "sacred" relationship between man and environment.

There is no doubt, as Martin and others contend, that Native Americans were the principal agents in overharvesting furbearers during the fur trade, but reasons for this activity have been misconstrued. As Martin points out, analysis of the fur trade and Native participation by means of western economic theory is a fruitless pastime. Western conceptions of markets and incentives cannot be usefully imposed upon culturally distinct groups. Martin prefers the notion that "traditional" time-honored religious systems were undermined and this led to Native American involvement in the trade. Without the long-standing religious ties to animals, Native Americans were lured into the trade because of the incentives that were provided by Europeans in the form of trade goods. Native Americans were not "seduced" into the trade; rather, the disintegration of cultural systems provided an appropriate environment in which the trade could occur. Once the trade cycle began, and Native peoples came to rely on European trade goods, indigenous practices and material culture fell into disuse. This, when coupled with the tremendous effects of disease upon Native populations, tied Native peoples to the trade in order to sustain themselves.

There are a number of assumptions that seriously flaw *Keepers of the Game*. In many instances, Martin takes his sources at face value, without critical appraisal. This is particularly true of his discussion of the Midewiwin (Grand Medicine Society of the Ojibwa). Martin agrees with Harold Hickerson "that the Midewiwin was a post-contact, nativistic cult."[20] He supports Hickerson's interpretation because Hickerson, who "has combed the *Jesuit Relations* and other appropriate seventeenth-century sources, found no signs of it prior to the early eighteenth century."[21] This interpretation is highly ethnocentric and denies the oral traditions of Native peoples, particularly the Ojibwa, which Martin sees fit to use when they suit his purposes. To disavow the existence of a highly secret society because it is not mentioned in the literature when that society functions in an oral culture, is a bias that contemporary historians must address. Emphasis on the quantification of literary sources detracts from the examination of culturally viable phenomena. Oral traditions of the Ojibwa place the Midewiwin in the precontact period. This has also been stated in the literature written by Native Americans.[22]

Martin's work is also marred by his inadequate knowledge of animals, particularly the beaver. Referring to the relationship between man and beaver, Martin states: "The two were locked in mortal combat, with the Indian the perennial underdog. Man's primitive tools were pitifully inadequate to penetrate the fortress-like lodge, reasoned [David] Thompson. So the Indian stood by and watched, helplessly, as beaver multiplied and became a nuisance, and then a menace, assuming possession of every waterway that lent itself to their purposes."[23] Martin goes on to cite a conversation between two Cree hunters during the late eighteenth or early nineteenth century (recorded by Thompson in his *Narrative*)[24] to provide evidence for the spiritual sanction for destruction of the beaver. One of the elder Cree spokesmen stated: "The Great Spirit has been, and now is, very angry with them and they are now all to be destroyed."[25] Martin uses this statement, which seems to be a classic rationalization for decimating beaver during the peak of the fur trade, as support for the contention "that on the eve of European contact man and beast were at war."[26] This proposal entirely denies the beaver's beneficial role in the Native hunter's ecosystem.

The beaver, within its aquatic environment, is a blessing to the hunter. The beaver's backwaters, from the construction of dams, support fish populations and provide habitat for other water mammals. Migrating waterfowl use beaver ponds for stop-overs, and in the spring the beaver marshes are prime nesting areas. Beaver dams provide major causeways for mammals, which allow the trapper prime spots to catch game, and, more important, the beaver ponds have the effect of funneling deer and other land animals into narrow spots where they can be taken by concealed hunters at close range.

In the northern beaver range, they provide the perfect habitat for moose, which can be hunted from the land or the water, using a canoe. The beaver may have been viewed as having fallen into disfavor with the Great Spirit during the peak of the fur trade, so as to rationalize the negation of traditional human-animal relations, but in the pre-contact world, and the post-fur-trade period, Native American hunters viewed the beaver as an ally. This is especially true when the beaver-human relationship in the pre-fur-trade period is examined, and when the effects of other forms of natural predation are considered. The beaver was, and is, preyed upon by wolves, lynx, wolverines, otters, bears, and coyotes, not to mention eagles, great horned owls, and hawks, which will attack the young. The beaver, in the natural ecosystem, was never perceived as a "nuisance" and most certainly never infringed on human landholdings.

Martin's explanation of the role of tularemia as a catalyst to the destruction of animals by Native hunters is equally unsupported. Tularemia, a bacterial disease, is thought to have been present on the North American continent in the "type A" strain, which is associated with land organisms, and in "type B," which is the less virulent form associated with wetlands.[27] The "type B" form would be the bacteria strain most likely to affect the beaver. Martin says this disease is fatal in less than one percent of the untreated cases in humans. He concludes after his discussion of tularemia, without citing any accounts of Native peoples attributing the causes of their sickness to animals, that:

> Speculation and conjecture aside, it is obvious that the Eastern Canadian and other North American Indians blamed wildlife for their diseases precisely because they were, indeed, the source of many of their ailments.[28]

This statement is in opposition to the historic perception of animals by Native peoples, and does not accurately reflect the causes of illness among tribes in the eastern woodlands.

William C. Sturtevant, in his critical essay on Martin's text, states that "there appears to be no evidence that northern Indians blamed wildlife in this way; rather, they blamed themselves for contravening the rules governing the relations between humans and animals."[29] Sickness in the native cosmology—as clarified by Sturtevant, and further supported by A. I. Hallowell—is caused by the behaviors of peoples. Hallowell contends that "any serious illness is associated with some prior conduct which involved an infraction of moral rules: the illness is explained as a penalty for bad conduct."[30] Even if Martin's assumption was correct about the causes of illness among eastern Canadian Indians, it would be a quantum leap in logic to infer that a disease that is fatal in less than one percent of the untreated cases was associated as the causal agent of pandemics which destroyed up to ninety percent of the members of certain Native American groups. Native peoples had absolutely no reason to attribute the effect of European diseases and the least virulent form of tularemia to the beaver.

The primary reason for my criticism of *Keepers of the Game* is to point out that Martin's consideration of Native peoples as non-conservationists is based on incorrect assumptions. He states in the concluding paragraph of *Keepers of the Game:* "Nature, for virtually all North American Indians, was sensate, animate, and capable of aggressive behavior toward mankind."[31] Martin was only partially correct. The environment was sensate and animate, and it was capable of inflicting harm, but animals were not the purveyors of these ill-tidings. Martin erroneously surmised that qualities of the environment predisposed Native peoples to "wage war" on animals, and this is simply not true.

Martin's underestimation of Native peoples is clearly exhibited in his inability to understand man-animal relations and the performance of condolences or rituals of atonement. Native peoples conducted rituals of atonement to assist the slain animal's spirit to the next world, and to give thanks for providing food for the hunter's family. This ritual was perceived as being a renewal of the formal ties of man and animal, and an acknowledgement of each respective party's role in the Creation. Native peoples conducted these atonements because they desired to dwell on the serious nature of their behavior. They had just killed another being to ensure the survival of their family, and this was a part of the Creator's will. Animals were gifts to man, and this relationship must be taken seriously. These rituals were not conducted, as Martin contends, to stop animals from "inflicting disease."[32] Martin's proposal that these rituals were only performed as protective devices would, of course, negate any ethical ties that Native hunters may have had with game animals. These ethical ties are the cornerstone of modern conservation, and Martin's inability to perceive atonements as anything other than protective measures forces him to pigeon-hole Native peoples as non-conservationists. There can be no doubt that western game animal populations would have fared much better if non-Indian hunters would have ritualized their actions of killing, or simply reflected on their ethical tie with the Creation, as Native hunters did.

Even when the Utes of Colorado killed thousands of antelope for their hides and meat in 1878, it was not a wanton act of destruction but a vehicle for the Utes to maintain some semblance of equality between themselves and the encroaching settlers and the military. By that date the buffalo were scarce on the northern plains, and Ute subsistence patterns were severely disrupted. They, as a people, were faced with minimal alternatives to ensure their continued survival. They could be exterminated or confined to reservations, or they could provide for themselves by hide-hunting. They chose the latter.

Some scholars have used examples of Native American complicity in acts of destruction to rationalize the conduct of non-Indian hunters. John F. Reiger states, for instance, that "it appears that the Indian, once corrupted, could give up his customary reverence for nature and exploit it just as ruthlessly as the white man."[33] Reiger and others neglect the effects of primarily non-Indian resource exploitation on Indian actions.

The actions of western settlers and hunters belie the absence of a land ethic or conservationist thought during the period 1870 to 1900. If land or environmental philosophies were considered, they were not popularly practiced by the "frontiersman."

In contrast to the frontier people, Native Americans have been identified as having and practicing a philosophical/spiritual tie with the land and with animal populations. This relationship remained intact during the decades of 1870–1900, and no other group of people decried the extermination of the American bison more than Native Americans. Prefatory remarks at many treaty councils between the federal government and Indian nations included statements that protested the destruction of game animals. With the elimination of food sources, indigenous peoples were forced to become more dependent upon the federal government. The resulting cultural disruption and change caused innumerable problems for Native peoples.

The frequent contact between American Indians and military personnel, guides, settlers, and travelers was destined to result in acculturation. Acculturation is the process of modifying culture via contact between differing groups. It is not a unilateral phenomenon. Some people assume that acculturation only affects the "primitive" or lesser developed groups when cultural contact occurs. This is simply not the case. Numerous examples can be cited which support the contention that acculturation is a two-way street. The adoption of tobacco by European populations, the reliance of early colonial settlers on corn and bean crops that were indigenous to North America, the utilization of Native American modes of transportation (canoe, snowshoes, toboggans), and the acquisition of Native American hunting techniques are examples of the acculturation of European populations to indigenous cultural patterns. The influences of Native peoples on the development of the North American continent are undeniable. It is not a preposterous assumption, then, that the philosophy of Native Americans should eventually have an impact on American perceptions of the natural world.

An earlier version of this essay appeared in *Northeast Indian Quarterly* 7 (Summer 1990): 3–13.

GEORGE L. CORNELL, an Ojibwa Indian living in Williamston, Michigan, is Associate Professor in English and American Studies at Michigan State University, where he also directs the Native American Institute. His doctoral dissertation at Michigan State focused on "Native American Contributions to the Formation of the Modern Conservation Ethic." He holds a B.S. and an M.A., both in psychology, from the same university. A former McNickle Fellow at the Newberry Library, he has published and lectured widely on Native American culture, with articles and papers on the Native American land ethic, literature, pow wows, treaties, Viet Nam, and many other topics. Through the Native American Institute, he has provided technical and grants writing assistance to Michigan Indian tribes and organizations.

Before and after fighting in the Viet Nam War, he was a professional drag racer.

Notes

1. Clark Wissler, *Indians of the United States* (New York, 1949), 301.

2. Alvin M. Josephy, Jr., *The Indian Heritage of America* (New York, 1968)., 12.

3. Robert F. Berkhofer, Jr., *The White Man's Indian: Images of the American Indian from Columbus to the Present* (New York, 1978), 4–5.

4. Adrian Tanner, *Bringing Home Animals: Indigenous Ideology and Mode of Production of the Mistassina Cree Hunters* (New York, 1979), 173.

5. Christopher Vecsey and Robert W. Venables, eds., *American Indian Environments* (Syracuse, 1980), x.

6. William A. Starna, review of *American Indian Environments*, in *American Anthropologist* 84 (1984).

7. Starna, 469.

8. Oren Lyons, "An Iroquois Perspective," in Vecsey and Venables, 174.

9. John M. Rich, *Chief Seattle's Unanswered Challenge* (Fairfield, Washington, 1970), 32–41.

10. *Shalom for the Land* (Minneapolis, n.d.), unpaginated.

11. Rich, 45.

12. John G. Neihardt, *Black Elk Speaks* (New York, 1972), 230.

13. J.R. Walker, *The Sun Dance and Other Ceremonies of the Oglala Division of the Teton Sioux* (New York, 1971), 160.

14. Barre Toelken, "Seeing With A Native Eye: How Many Sheep Will It Hold?" in *Seeing With a Native Eye: Essays on Native American Religion* edited by Walter Holden Capps (New York, 1976), 14.

15. William Carlos Williams, *In the American Grain* (New York, 1925).

16. Cy Martin, *The Saga of the Buffalo* (New York, 1973), 138.

17. Cy Martin, 94.

18. Cy Martin, 170.

19. Calvin Martin, *Keepers of the Game: Indian-Animal Relationships and the Fur Trade* (Los Angeles and Berkeley, 1973), 157.

20. Calvin Martin, 85.

21. Calvin Martin, 85.

22. Edward Benton-Benai, *The Mishomis Book: The Voice of the Ojibway* (St. Paul, 1979), 94–102.

23. Calvin Martin, 106.

24. David Thompson, *Narrative, 1784–1812*, edited by Richard Glober (Toronto, 1962).

25. Calvin Martin, 107.

26. Calvin Martin, 107.

27. Calvin Martin, 141.

28. Calvin Martin, 144.

29. William C. Sturtevant, "Animals and Disease in Indian Belief," in *Indians, Animals, and the Fur Trade: A Critique of Keepers of the Game,* edited by Shepard Krech, III (Athens, GA, 1981), 180.

30. Sturtevant, 183.

31. Calvin Martin, 187.

32. Calvin Martin, 82.

33. John R. Reiger, *The Passing of the Great West: Selected Papers of George Bird Grinnell* (New York, 1972), 141.

Suggestions for Further Reading

Capps, Walter H., ed. *Seeing with a Native Eye: Essays on Native American Religion*. New York: Harper Forum Books, 1976.

Clifton, James, George Cornell, and J. McClurken. *People of the Three Fires*. Grand Rapids, MI: Grand Rapids Inter-Tribal Council, 1986.

Cornell, George L., "American Indian Philosophy and Perceptions of the Environment." In *Human Values and the Environment*, edited by Faith B. Miracle, pp. 41–46. Madison: Wisconsin Academy of Sciences, Arts and Letters, Report 140, 1992.

Cornell, George L., "The Influence of Native Americans on Modern Conservation," *Environmental Review* 9, 2 (1985): 104–17.

Cornell, George L., "Native Americans and Environmental Thought: Thoreau and the Transcendentalists," in *Akwe:kon* (formerly *Northeast Indian Quarterly*) 9.3 (1992): 4–13.

Crosby, Alfred W. *Ecological Imperialism: The Biological Expansion of Europe, 900–1900*. New York: Cambridge University Press, 1986.

Hughes, J. Donald. *American Indian Ecology*. El Paso: Texas Western Press, 1983.

Hultkrantz, Ake. *Native Religions of North America*. New York: Harper and Row, 1987.

Huth, Hans. *Nature and the American: Three Centuries of Changing Attitudes*. Lincoln: University of Nebraska Press, Bison Books, 1972.

Lopez, Barry H. *Of Wolves and Men*. New York: Charles Scribner's Sons, 1978.

Matthiessen, Peter. *Wildlife in America*. New York: Viking Press, 1959.

Sayre, Robert F. *Thoreau and the American Indians*. Princeton: Princeton University Press, 1977.

Chippewa Lodge by Seth Eastman. Ojibwa women are constructing bark-covered wigwams. From *Information Respecting the History, Condition and Prospects of the United States*, 6 volumes, Henry Rowe Schoolcraft (Philadelphia: Lippincott, Grambo & Co., 1851–1857). Photo courtesy State Historical Society of Wisconsin. WHi(X3)34131.

Spearing Fish in Winter by Seth Eastman. This mid-nineteenth century illustration depicts a method of fishing still followed by some Ojibwa bands. The spearer lays on pine boughs or a blanket. A blanket-covered frame limits external light while the spearer tries to entice fish within spearing range by jigging a decoy in the hole he has augured through the ice. Photo courtesy State Historical Society of Wisconsin. WHi(X3)13551.

Pictographs on Lake Superior and Carp River, Michigan, drawn by Seth Eastman. From *Information Respecting the History, Condition and Prospects of the Indian Tribes of the United States,* 6 volumes, Henry Rowe Schoolcraft (Philadelphia: Lippincott, Grambo & Co., 1851–1857). Photo courtesy State Historical Society of Wisconsin. WHi(X3)34133.

Ojibwa women harvesting wild rice. Engraving from a drawing by Seth Eastman, from *American Aboriginal Portfolio*, Mary Eastman, 1953. Photo courtesy State Historical Society of Wisconsin. WHi(X3)25013.

Ojibwa wild rice harvesters, Lake Mille Lacs, Minnesota. Photo courtesy State Historical Society of Wisconsin. WHi(X3)28608.

Ojibwa woman preparing ash splints for basket making, ca. 1925. Photo courtesy State Historical Society of Wisconsin. WHi(X3)18837.

Ojibwa burial ground with spirit houses, Lac Courte Oreilles Ojibwa reservation. Photo courtesy State Historical Society of Wisconsin. WHi(W63)2938.

Lac Courte Oreilles Ojibwa Reservation. Photo courtesy State Historical Society of Wisconsin. WHi(W63)2943.

Lac Courte Oreilles Ojibwa School near Hayward, Wisconsin, ca. 1882–1886. Photo courtesy State Historical Society of Wisconsin. WHi(X3)23295.

Trickster:

A Compendium

Kimberly M. Blaeser

University of Wisconsin–Milwaukee

I heard a story once about an encounter between Pablo Picasso and a United States sailor. Picasso, as many of you know, was a Spanish artist famous for, among other things, his cubist creations, works which might, for example, portray the human face disjointedly in a mosaic form, one eye here, bits of various colored shapes adjacent to it, and down lower another eye. Anyway, this sailor asked Picasso in a somewhat self-righteous tone, "Why do you paint people in this way? People don't really look like that!" Now, Picasso was an artist in many ways. In response to this criticism of his work, he simply shrugged in a self-effacing way and shifted the conversation around to the sailor and the sailor's life, and, finding out the sailor had a girlfriend, he asked to see a picture of her. The sailor proudly pulled out his wallet and showed Picasso a snapshot. Picasso studied the picture, turned it this way and that, held it up close, held it at arm's length, then finally asked the sailor, "Is this a good likeness of her?" The sailor assured him it was a good picture of his girlfriend: "It looks just like her," he said. "Really," said Picasso, as if surprised. Then, looking again at the photo and gesturing a little with his hands, he asked, "You mean she is truly so small?" Yes, Picasso was an artist.

I use this story today because it seems to me that talking *about* Trickster, analyzing him, summarizing the characteristics and purposes of trickster tales (which is our task today), is reductive in the same way that a photograph is reductive. A photograph gives us an image of something, an idea of what something is like, but even if it is a very good likeness, it is but one view, a flat one-dimensional image of the reality. And so, as we speak of Trickster today, you must try to blow life into the image, to imagine Trickster as life energy, to allow Trickster to step out of the verbal photograph we create.

In contemplating my remarks for today, considering the magnitude of our subject, the long tradition of trickster tales, the tribal variations that exist, the multitude of things that could and have been said about the trickster figure, I began to worry first about having too much to say and then, when I began to finally put my thoughts together, about not having enough to say that hasn't been said before. Finally, I realized that although my own reading in preparation for this conference covered a lot of ground that I have covered before, it still seemed new. In reading the stories I still would be brought to laughter (sometimes in rather inappropriate situations). And in trying to characterize the trickster figure, I would find myself as baffled as if I had never encountered the character before. It was then I realized why Trickster remains a vital part of tribal literature and tradition, so much so that a state-wide conference would be dedicated to the subject. Why? Because trickster stories still have power: the power to bring us to laughter, the power to baffle us, the power to make us wonder and think and, like Trickster, just keep going on.

So it is about these things that I would like to talk today: about the history and tradition of Trickster, about the character of the trickster figure (what we think we know and what we realize we can never finally know about this ambiguous figure), about the purposes and functions of trickster tales (why we tell them, what they contribute to our lives and society), and, finally, about the

mysterious persistence of trickster literature, the survival of traditional trickster stories, and the ongoing incorporation of Trickster
into contemporary tribal literature. I call this a compendium because it truly is an abridged version, a mere sketch of or introduction to many of the traits and functions of trickster tales, each of
which could yield (and some of which have yielded) an entire
study themselves. So with no further qualifications I begin the
compendium.

History and Tradition

Coyote, Raven, Spider, Blue Jay, Dragonfly, Raccoon, Hare, Wol-
verine or Old Man Coyote, Naanabozho, Toe'osh, Iktome, Pehrru,
Wakdjunkaga, Nanabush. The names of the trickster figure have
been numerous, as have the associations made between trickster
and certain animal forms. Names, associations, and to some extent,
characteristics of the figure, as well as the stories themselves, vary
from tribe to tribe, but the metaphorical energy that is Trickster has
surfaced in myth throughout North America and in related mythic
figures in South America and in other parts of the world. The Monkey King of China, the shape-shifting fox of Japanese culture, Brer
Rabbit of African folk tales, the mythic Khoja of Turkish legend, all
these characters embody trickster energy, as do many related figures in contemporary culture like Bugs Bunny or the Road Runner.[1]
But even in an abridged form I couldn't possibly hope to deal with
all these manifestations. So in my comments today, I restrict myself to generalizations about the trickster figure among Native
American Indian peoples (acknowledging at the start that they are
generalizations and that individual tribes understood trickster energy in slightly varying ways).

The trickster figure appears in the oral literature of a great number of tribes: the Blackfoot, the Klamath, the Navajo, the Crow, the
Modoc, the Salish, the Winnebago, the Lakota, the Ojibway, and a
multitude of others. Often the stories are a part of a cycle of tales
and, in certain tribes including the Navajo and the Winnebago,
these tales include sacred stories: stories which can only be told at

certain times, by certain people, and only after specific ritual preparations have been made.

Within any one tribe's repertoire, the subjects and the tone of
the stories vary greatly. Some stories tell of the creation, or of the
origins of certain elements of the world like the sun, the moon,
the seasons, or death. Some serve a teaching role in tribal society,
upholding one kind of behavior or cautioning against another.
Some provide a release for frustrations stemming from social re-
strictions. Still others seem pure entertainment, telling of the outrageous antics of Trickster. The trickster character we meet in
these stories is itself various, changing—ambiguous. The compendium opens now to—

Ambiguous Characteristics

Gerald Vizenor, whom we will be honored to hear later this eve-
ning, made a statement about Trickster in one of his recent books,
The Trickster of Liberty, which seems to me to capture exactly the
ambiguity that pervades both the figure of trickster and any discussion of this literary figure: he likens the tribal trickster to "a warrior
on a coin that never lands twice on the same side."[2] Such a wild
image implies both the ambiguity and the vitality of Trickster.
Barre Toelken speaks of Trickster as "the exponent of all possibilities."[3] And indeed, he (or she) is that, as we shall see as we begin to
skim the list of qualities that characterize this mythic figure.

Perhaps one of the most basic and yet the most confounding questions about Trickster remains "What is he?" Is Trickster a coyote
(or any of the many other animal forms we mentioned)? Is Trickster
human? Is Trickster a god? The scholarly answer to this tells us that
Trickster is one of what are called the First People in Native American tradition, one of those who were in the world in mythic time,
before humans came to be here, and that, as one of these First People, Trickster is not distinctly human, animal, or god, but has magical powers, including the ability to change shape at will. So, as a
cultural figure, Trickster makes the transition from mythic to modern times and remains not fully one kind of being (animal, man, or

god). I said that was the scholarly answer, the academic answer; the metaphorical answer, the answer that tribal people as storytellers understand more readily than scholars, is that Trickster defies categorization, that he is both none and all three of these beings. Toelken makes an important distinction about the Navajo trickster, saying that "he is not a composite but a complex."[4] Not a composite, which is made up of distinct and recognizable parts, but a complex, which is one unit whose makeup is intricate and interwoven. Trickster resists classification and survives outside the boundaries of time. Trickster is a marginal figure, a mediator who breaks down any hard and fast distinctions. Trickster is . . . imaginative energy.

Neither wholly this, nor wholly that; acting sometimes this way, sometimes another way—Trickster ambiguities continue to add up. Trickster is neither solely good, nor solely bad; neither completely wise, nor only foolish; sometimes the wily perpetrator of tricks, sometimes the buffoon who falls victim to his own pride; sometimes the tribal benefactor, sometimes the bungler who spoils some aspect of the world for man. Or, as Jarold Ramsey has noted, Trickster may not be either/or, but simultaneously both. Ramsey speaks of Trickster and Trickster stories as "a dynamic interposing of the mind between polar opposites, allowing it to hold onto both opposites, as if affirming either/and."[5] Not either/or, but either/and: Trickster mediates between supposed contradictory forces or elements by retaining aspects of both, by revealing them to be coexisting parts of one whole, interconnected, often indistinguishable elements of the one. Ambiguity approaches truth in a way that clarity cannot.

For example, looking at a story which tells of Trickster preventing people from eliminating death from the world, we might first classify Trickster as a villainous bungler. But in the tale as told in one Caddo version, Trickster cautions the Indians who have plotted to overcome death: "But you forget one thing, oh wise ones. If folks keep right on being born, yet no one stays dead, the world will be a crowded place pretty soon. How are you going to feed all those people, oh wise ones? Where are you going to put them?"[6] So, is Trickster bungler or benefactor or, ambiguously, both? As we have noted, Trickster is all possibility.

For example, when Ramsey asks, "Of what is a . . . Trickster capable?" he answers:

> Anything, it appears from the evidence, anything, that is, that does not express consistent restraint or altruistic, responsibly domestic, or executive motives. Coyote . . . wanders around, masquerades, lies, steals, attempts to defraud, hoards, gorges himself, commits rape, masturbates, schemes to commit incest, seeks unwarranted revenges, wastes natural resources, plays malicious tricks, is dismembered, is swallowed whole, expelled, publicly humiliated—all the while inventing important rituals, naming and placing the tribes, chartering fishing rights, laying down laws of marriage, warfare, and so on, and establishing the permanence of death.[7]

Within this infinite range of possibilites, however, a few of Trickster's features can be pinned down. Trickster is most often characterized as a wanderer, always on the move. Trickster tales frequently begin with Coyote (or whichever character is being spoken of) in motion: "Coyote was walking with his friend," "Coyote was out hunting," "Coyote was paddling his canoe," "Coyote was going there," "Once Coyote was going visiting," "One day Coyote started out to. . . ."

And this peripatetic figure (who has been likened to the character of the *picaro* in the picaresque novelistic tradition) proves himself in the tales to be inquisitive, often reckless, but also adaptable and irrepressible. Ramsey speaks of his "predilection, one might say his genius, for always being in the middle, in all kinds of middles, in muddles."[8] Trickster links up with friends; he plots; he gambles; he sings, talks, and brags his way along; he breaks the rules just because they are there; he repeatedly indulges his gluttonous appetite for food and sex; and he laughs as heartily as he lives.

One of my favorite tales which shows Trickster in a characteristic encounter is the story of a cheating contest. Told by the Sioux as

"Coyote and Washichu," and here in a Kiowa version called "Coyote and the Stranger," this story also surfaces in other variations.

Coyote was going along one day, trotting down the desert way, when he saw the dust of a horse and rider.

White man coming! And look at the fancy rig on him!

Well, old Coyote was a shape shifter, of course. In no time, he had taken manshape, looking just like a poor man of the people, dark skin, black hair. Only his eyes were odd, the mocking green eyes of the trickster.

Did the stranger know him by those eyes? Maybe. For the man pointed right at Coyote and said, "Heard there's someone around here who fancies himself a cheater. Someone by the name of Coyote."

Cheater! Coyote thought indignantly. A fine name for someone who set the sun in the sky! "Might be," he answered smoothly, bland of face. But behind that blank mask, his busy mind was plotting.

"Ha, you're Coyote, I know it! But I'm a better cheater than you. Ain't a man alive who can out-trick me, surely not some worn-out Indian! Come on, try me!"

Now, here was a pretty bird, just asking to be plucked! Coyote grinned, lazily, tongue lolling out. "The day's too warm."

"Try me! Try to cheat me!"

"No. The sun's too hot."

"You're afraid! You're scared to have a cheating match with me."

Coyote sighed. "Trouble is, I left my cheating medicine back home."

"Well, go get it."

"It's too far. I'm too tired. You want a cheating match, better wait till another day. Or lend me your horse so I can get there and back again."

The stranger thought that one over just for a minute, so eager was he to show what a mighty trickster he was. He jumped down from the saddle. But Coyote slyly moved upwind of the horse.

And it, smelling the not-human scent of him, shied, eyes rolling, ears twitching.

"He's scared of me because I don't have a white man's hat," Coyote said. "Let me borrow yours."

"Here, take it. Go get your cheating medicine!"

But Coyote still stood upwind. And of course the horse still shied. Coyote shrugged. "He's scared of me because I don't wear a white man's clothes. Guess our match is off."

But the stranger was so eager to prove himself, he peeled out of his fancy shirt and pants and boots without a moment's thought. "Here, try them."

Coyote slid into the alien clothes, leaving the man only his long johns. With the alien hat on his head, Coyote moved downwind. Unable to scent him, the horse stood still. Coyote mounted and urged it into a trot. But then, safely out of reach, old Coyote reined in the horse again, looked back at the denuded man, and grinned.

"Well, stranger," he called. "Are you content? Learned your lesson?"

"Lesson? What are you talking about?"

"Look down at yourself, stranger. No clothes, no horse. Look down and admit: No man living can trick Coyote!"

The man's mouth dropped open as he realized how he'd been fooled. "Why you sly, no-good son of a—You come back here!" He raged.

But with a wave of his hand, Coyote rode away.[9]

But Trickster doesn't always escape or walk off laughing from his various escapades, sometimes he gets his comeuppance and slinks off or becomes a social outcast, and sometimes he dies—or perhaps we should say, is temporarily killed, for another of Trickster's characteristic qualities is his indestructibility. Ramsey calls him a "mythic survivor" and describes the multitude of ills Trickster does survive: "starvation, poisoning, dismemberment, ingestion by monsters, incineration, drowning, fatal falls, and so on."[10] But from these tortuous fates Trickster recovers, is revived, patches himself up and goes on his way, or he implicitly survives, appearing as he does in subsequent tales.

Why have Trickster and his tales been kept alive in the tribes? What explanations can be offered for the existence of similar tales among so many tribes? Why has such importance been placed on these generally lighthearted stories?

Functions of Trickster Tales

Enjoyable as they are for their own sake, the purposes of trickster tales go far beyond the entertainment derived from the accounts of the irrepressible personality and outlandish antics of Trickster. In ways both readily apparent and more subtly discernible, these tales serve the individual and societal needs of tribal people and contribute to cultural survival, acting as teaching tools, tools of liberation, and repositories of tribal history and tradition. I now turn to a discussion of several of these functions and to illuminating the dynamics of each.

Perhaps the most frequently noted purpose of trickster tales is their teaching dynamic. Obviously lessons are conveyed through the stories by example: Trickster learns lessons the hard way, we learn them the easy way, vicariously. Trickster tales frequently work to enlighten the audience to their own flaws or to caution against certain actions by exposing the ludicrousness of Trickster's actions. Barbara Babcock has termed this function of the tales "myth as social charter," with the trickster stories serving to reinforce the laws and customs of society.[11] Barre Toelken also talks about this aspect of the dynamics of trickster tales. He speaks specifically about the importance of the tales in establishing tribal values in children, and of their part in teaching children without the tedium of direct instruction:

In the tales one is struck by the presence of both humor and of those culture references against which the morality of Coyote's actions may be judged. . . . Causing children to laugh at an action because it is thought to be weak, stupid or excessive is to order their moral assessment of it without recourse to open explanation or didacticism.[12]

Of course, the lessons couched in trickster tales are for children and adults alike.

The fascinating aspect of this instructive function of the stories is that the performance of the tales manages to transform the learning process into a communal, joyful, active process. Trickster errs, we learn. The stories relate the faulty thinking of the trickster figure so that we may recognize the folly of our own erroneous thinking. Trickster saves us from mistakes by making them for us—in story. He teaches us how to think by learning how himself—in story. Engaged in the stories, we learn the lessons, and lessons presented with laughter are less resisted, more readily absorbed. As Black Elk says, "Truth comes into this world with two faces, one is sad with weeping, the other laughs, but it is the same face, laughing or weeping."[13] In trickster tales, truth enters laughing.

We see another level of the teaching function of the tales in their frequent use of satire, the presentation of a comic evaluation or reassessment of certain behavior or certain situations. Here rather than reinforcing established values, the stories often question the status quo (which, incidentally, is one of the functions that modern-day stories about Trickster perform most frequently). The purpose in early tribal culture was (as it is today) frequently political: to warn those holding power against acting powerful instead of acting like the mediators of power, or, as Ramsey notes, to warn against false customs and false Shamans.[14] A good example of a satirical attack on a contemporary situation is found in Jack Forbes's "Only Approved Indians Can Play: Made in the USA," which exposes the ludicrousness of tribal people adopting white BIA standards to measure their Indianness. Forbes's story implies that such actions ironically prove not authentic tribal identity, but instead testify to the success of assimilation policies.[15]

Another function of the tales related to satirical challenges of situations arising in tribal life (or challenges to the status quo) is the ability of trickster tales to help release the tensions or negative feelings that naturally arise when humans subject themselves to the rules and customs of community. As Trickster free-wheels his way through life, blatantly transgressing rules, customs, and good sense, all those touched by the stories enjoy an imaginative escape from the enforced structures of society. This saturnalian function of trickster stories Babcock calls "a social steam valve"[16]—it is an acceptable means of releasing tension and thus, ultimately, safeguards the very values and customs Trickster himself undermines in story. Ramsey explains that these tales "allowed the 'good citizens' of the tribe to affirm the system of prohibitions and punishments that the Trickster chronically runs afoul of—at the same time that they could vicariously delight and find release in his irresponsible individualism."[17] We are in a sense liberated from the tensions and frustrations we may have otherwise sublimated.

Trickster also liberates in another, even more crucial way. Babcock speaks of a "reflective-creative function" of trickster tales and the creation of "communitas"—a state in which social distinctions are leveled.[18] Other scholars, Gerald Vizenor being one of the most prominent, have also spoken of this important dynamic of the trickster tradition. Essentially what occurs is this: the tales, as we have noted, give our tightly patterned thinking and the status quo a "dressing down"; they reveal the artificial nature of divisions and of social structure, and they reveal the arbitrary and subjective nature of many of our established perceptions. We realize there is no final, ultimate answer, no infallibility that we can blindly accept and follow. Power, like life, is in motion. So, recognizing what Babcock calls the "as-if nature of social forms and structures,"[19] we experience a new sense of freedom. Our illusion of order gives way to a new recognition of our individual power and freedom. It is this new state of liberation that engenders creativity, imagination, life energies.

And such an awakening to possibility is precisely the function of trickster tales that has endured and continues to ensure tribal survival. William Bright says about the trickster figure: "Coyote has . . . been around a long time; he has seen everything and tried everything—and if he has not learned everything, he has surely learned that the key to survival is to keep trying."[20] And Jarold Ramsey, speaking of the mediative function of Trickster says, "Mediation does not mean 'compromise and reconciliation'. . . . It is a continuing process of the mind, not a transitional step toward some conclusion."[21] What both of these statements point to is the recognition of the prerequisite to survival—continuance, not submission to defeat, not even triumph, for both are only temporary. If I may borrow another quote from Jerry Vizenor: "The ritual of a spider building its web on the wind. . . . That is survival!"[22] And so we continue, and so the stories continue.

Trickster Survives through the Ages

Trickster stories and trickster energy do survive, as clearly evidenced in the work of oral historians and contemporary tribal writers alike. Traditional trickster stories continue to be told and to find their way into new and better translations. And contemporary writers keep alive the tradition—Gerald Vizenor, Leslie Silko, Simon Ortiz, Louise Erdrich, Peter Blue Cloud, and many others. Often their work is a blend of the old with the new, showing the continued vitality and relevance of tradition today. Here, for example, is a trickster poem by Silko which blends the past and present in the continuum of the now:

Toe'osh: A Laguna Coyote Story

In the wintertime
at night
we tell coyote stories
                and drink Spañada by the stove.
How coyote got his
ratty old fur coat
                bits of old fur
                the sparrows stuck on him
                with dabs of pitch.

That was after he lost his proud original one in a poker game.
anyhow, things like that
are always happening to him,
that's what he said, anyway.

And it happened to him at Laguna
and Chinle
and at Lukachukai too, because coyote got too smart for his own good.

But the Navajos say he won a contest once.
It was to see who could sleep out in a
snowstorm the longest
and coyote waited until chipmunk badger and skunk were all
curled up under the snow
and then he uncovered himself and slept all night
inside
and before morning he got up and went out again
and waited until the others got up before he came
in to take the prize.

Some white men came to Acoma and Laguna a hundred years ago
and they fought over Acoma land and Laguna women, and even now
some of their descendants are howling in
the hills southeast of Laguna.

Charlie Coyote wanted to be governor
and he said that when he got elected
he would run the other men off
the reservation
and keep all the women for himself.

One year
the politicians got fancy
at Laguna.
They went door to door with hams and turkeys
and they gave them to anyone who promised
to vote for them.
On election day all the people
stayed home and ate turkey
and laughed.

The Trans-Western pipeline vice president came
to discuss right-of-way.
The Lagunas let him wait all day long
because he is a busy and important man.
And late in the afternoon they told him
to come back again tomorrow.

They were after the picnic food
that the special dancers left
down below the cliff.
And Toe'osh and his cousins hung themselves
down over the cliff
holding each other's tail in their mouth making a coyote chain
until someone in the middle farted
and the guy behind him opened his
mouth to say "What stinks?" and they
all went tumbling down, like that.

Howling and roaring
Toe'osh scattered white people
out of bars all over Wisconsin.
He bumped into them at the door
until they said,
                    "Excuse me"
And the way Simon meant it
was for 300 or maybe 400 years.[23]

Yes, Trickster is, as Ramsey claims, a "mythic survivor," and the stories help assure tribal survival as well.

In closing, I would like to offer two things: a disclaimer and a story. Toelken acknowledges that Trickster has "consistently evaded academic capture and definition and has tricked nearly every commentator into at least one outrageous and laughable generalization."[24] I feel certain I too must fall amid this company, but I take heart, for if I have been outwitted, it is by the supreme Trickster.

And finally, one more story:

Trickster Meets the Would-be Intellectuals

One day Naanabozho was walking along thinking about nothing but how warm the sun felt and whom he would visit to get his lunch. Soon he came to a lodge very much like this one and he saw a lot of cars and people and thought to himself, "Ah, these people must be gathering because they have something good to eat." You see Naanabozho was much more practical than we are today and couldn't have conceived of gathering around to listen to someone talk for hours at a time unless there was also gambling or food or drink. So he decided to go into the lodge and see what he could find.

But when he got to the door he saw a sign that said, "Shirt and Shoes Required." Well at first Naanabozho thought that a snow-shoe like himself might get by by just liberating a shirt somewhere, but then he looked at the people there and saw the kind of shoes they were wearing and, well, he changed his mind. Anyway, Naanabozho, you know, was pretty much of a braggart, so much so that sometimes he even bragged to himself. Well that's what happened this time. "A sly fellow like me," he said to himself, "I can certainly come up with a fine pair of shoes and a shirt that will put these scruffy humans to shame." So he sat down on the curb and gave it some thought. He probably would have come up with something pretty good, too, but all that walking had tired him out, so before long he fell asleep.

Naanabozho had been sleeping soundly, dreaming of deer meat and fry-bread, when all of a sudden he felt a pain in his side and he opened his eyes to see some little public enemies standing there staring at him and one of them had a sharp stick with which he kept poking the trickster. "Hey, hey there! You cut that out!" shouted Naanabozho.

"See I told you he was alive," said the stick-holder. "You can't get a rabbit's foot off a live rabbit. It'll bleed all over you."

Now this of course gave Naanabozho an idea. "You want a rabbit's foot?"

"Yeah, it's good luck. But they cost a quarter."

Now Naanabozho was admittedly a little put out that people placed such an insignificant price on a fine specimen of a foot like his, but about this time his hunger was getting fierce and so he pretended it didn't bother him. "I'll trade you," he said.

"Hmmn?"

"I'll trade you my foot for your shoes and that shirt your friend is wearing."

Now like all little kids, these two knew their parents. Parents might be *min-da-we*[25] for a while about the loss of a pair of shoes or a shirt, but even if they wouldn't shell out a measly quarter for something important like a rabbit's foot, they would never let their children go without clothes and shoes. "Okay, it's a deal." And they each spit in their hands and held them out to Naanabozho.

And soon Naanabozho was wearing a pair of grade-A Nikes and a Teenage Mutant Ninja Turtle T-shirt. "Okay, hand it over."

"Huh?"

"The foot, hand it over."

"Oh, but I just got these shoes all laced up and I'm in a hurry. You wait here and I'll give it to you on my way out."

"Alright, but don't you try to welsh on our deal."

With that the two public enemies, one barefoot and one bare-chested sat down with great determination on the curb and watched Naanabozho go inside. You know, don't you, that they would wait a very long time?

Inside the lodge, Naanabozho saw a bunch of people sitting around a very large table and he tried to get closer to see what good things they had to eat. But when he finally squeezed his way up close enough to see, he saw nothing but a bunch of papers before each one. Naanabozho, disgusted with their strange appetites, was about to leave and continue his search for real food, but the lace of one of his new shoes caught on a nail and the shoe pulled off his foot.

Then it happened, one of the people recognized him, and before Naanabozho could even think up a good story to tell, he found himself on the center of the table, being examined and picked apart by the group of intellectuals. Poor Naanabozho! he lay there dazed, each of his parts being held up and stretched all out of proportion by members of the group. He thought this was truly the end of him and his magic this time.

Then a funny thing happened. The men and women became hypnotized by their own voices. Soon Naanabozho's parts lay abandoned and scattered about the table, and the people seemed to have forgotten him, so involved were they in making their fancy words better and louder than those of all the other intellectuals. So Naanabozho quietly shaped the pieces of paper to look like his different parts, then, gathering himself together as best he could, he crawled out of there.

When he was putting his foot back on, he remembered the deal he had made with the kids outside. So he climbed out of a window and off he went thinking to himself, "If only I can find someone who will trade me something good to eat for this shirt and these shoes. . . ."

And that's why intellectuals even today have only words on paper while the real Trickster is still wandering about out there—laughing!

KIMBERLY M. BLAESER, an Anishinaabe and an enrolled member of the Minnesota Chippewa Tribe, grew up on the White Earth Reservation. Currently an associate professor in the English and Comparative Literature Department at the University of Wisconsin–Milwaukee, she teaches twentieth-century American literature, including courses in Native American Literature and American Nature Writing. Blaeser's publications include poetry, short fiction, personal essays, journalism, and scholarly articles. Her poetry collection, *Trailing You,* won the 1993 Native Writers' Circle of the Americas First Book Award and her book *Gerald Vizenor: Writing in the Oral Tradition* is forthcoming from the University of Oklahoma Press.

Notes

1. For additional information on the manifestations of trickster in various cultures and in contemporary culture, see *The World and I* 5. 4 (1990): 614–69.

2. Gerald Vizenor, *The Trickster of Liberty* (Minneapolis, 1988), xviii.

3. "Foreward," *Giving Birth to Thunder, Sleeping with His Daughter: Coyote Builds North America,* edited by Barry Lopez (Kansas City, 1977), xii.

4. Barre Toelken, "Ma'i Joldloshi: Legendary Styles and Navajo Myth," in *American Folk Legend,* edited by W. Hand (Berkeley, 1971), 203.

5. Jarold Ramsey, "Coyote and Friends: An Experiment in Interpretative Bricolage," in *Reading the Fire: Essays in the Traditional Indian Literatures of the Far West* (Lincoln, 1983), 29.

6. Josepha Sherman, "Child of Chaos; Coyote: A Folkloric Tradition," *The World and I* 5.4 (1990): 648.

7. Ramsey, 26.

8. Ramsey, 28.

9. Sherman, 649–50. Sherman's article appeared in the April 1990 issue of *The World and I* and is reprinted with permission from *The World and I,* a publication of The Washington Times Corporation, copyright © 1990.

10. Ramsey, 42.

11. Barbara Babcock, " 'A Tolerated Margin of Mess': The Trickster and His Tales Reconsidered," in *Critical Essays on Native American Literature,* edited by Andrew Wiget (Boston, 1985), 179.

12. Toelken, "The 'Pretty Languages' of Yellowman: Genre, Mode, and Texture in Navajo Coyote Narratives," in *Folklore Genres,* edited by Dan Ben-Amos (Austin, 1976), 161–62.

13. John G. Neihardt, *Black Elk Speaks: Being the Life and Story of a Holy Man of the Oglala Sioux* (New York, 1932; 1975), 159.

14. Ramsey, 33.

15. Jack Forbes, "Only Approved Indians Can Play: Made in the USA," in *Earth Power Coming: Short Fiction in Native American Literature,* edited by Simon J. Ortiz (Tsaile, Arizona, 1983), 263–63.

16. Babcock, 180.

17. Ramsey, 32.

18. Babcock, 180–81.

19. Babcock, 181.

20. William Bright, "The Natural History of Old Man Coyote," in *Recovering the Word: Essays on Native American Literature*, edited by Brian Swann and Arnold Krupat (Berkeley, 1987), 376.

21. Ramsey, 29.

22. Vizenor, *Darkness in St. Louis Bearheart* (St. Paul, 1978), 187.

23. Leslie Silko, "Toe'osh: A Laguna Coyote Story." Copyright © 1981 by Leslie Marmon Silko. Reprinted from *Storyteller* by Leslie Marmon Silko, published by Seaver Brothers, New York, New York.

24. Toelken, "Foreword," *Giving Birth to Thunder*, xi.

25. An Ojibwa word meaning mad or annoyed.

Suggestions for Further Reading

Babcock, Barbara. " 'A Tolerated Margin of Mess': The Trickster and His Tales Reconsidered." In *Critical Essays on Native American Literature*, edited by Andrew Wiget, pp. 153–85. Boston: G. K. Hall, 1985.

Bright, William. "The Natural History of Old Man Coyote." In *Recovering the Word: Essays on Native American Literature*, edited by Brian Swann and Arnold Krupat, pp. 339–87. Berkeley: University of California Press, 1987.

Danker, Kathleen A. "Because of This I Am Called the Foolish One: Felix White, Sr.'s Interpretations of the Winnebago Trickster." In *New Voices in Native American Literary Criticism*, edited by Arnold Krupat, pp. 505–28. Washington: Smithsonian Institution Press, 1993.

Erdoes, Richard, and Alfonso Ortiz, eds. *American Indian Myths and Legends*. New York: Pantheon Books, 1985.

Koller, James. 'Gogisgi' Carroll Arnett, Steve Nemirow, and Peter Blue Cloud. *Coyote's Journal*. Berkeley: Wingbow Press, 1982.

Lincoln, Kenneth. "Old Tricks, New Twists." In *Indi'n Humor: Bicultural Play in Native America*, pp. 132–52. New York: Oxford University Press, 1993.

Lopez, Barry Holstun. *Giving Birth to Thunder, Sleeping With His Daughter: Coyote Builds North America.* Kansas City: Sheed Andrews and McMeel, 1977. Includes foreword by Barre Toelken.

Radin, Paul. *The Trickster: A Study in American Indian Mythology.* New York: Greenwood Press, 1969; New York: Schocken, 1987.

Ramsey, Jarold. *Coyote Was Going There: Indian Literature of the Oregon Country.* Seattle: University of Washington Press, 1977.

Wiget, Andrew. "His Life in His Tail: The Native American Trickster and the Literature of Possibility." In *Redefining American Literary History,* edited by A. LaVonne Brown Ruoff and Jerry W. Ward, pp. 83–96. New York: Modern Language Association of America, 1990.

Trickster Discourse:

Comic and Tragic Themes in Native American Literature

Gerald Vizenor

University of California–Berkeley

"We are what we imagine. Our very existence consists in our imagination of ourselves. Our best destiny is to imagine, at least, completely, who and what, and *that* we are. The greatest tragedy that can befall us is to go unimagined," said N. Scott Momaday at the First Convocation of American Indian Scholars.[1]

We are sustained in stories, by the natural reason of our imagination, but the tragedy "to go unimagined" has dominated most interpretations of tribal remembrance. What might have been imagined has too often been buried in the monologues of dominance.

My argument is that tribal cultures have been largely unimagined by the social sciences. And this is the second or third time since the dubious discoveries of Christopher Columbus that Native American Indians have been the sources of national and political imagination. The difference in the past couple of decades is that Native Americans are imagining themselves. This is a powerful source of consciousness, identity, and presentation in the world. And if any of us doubt the power of such stories that arise from imagination, surely half of us must be here because of imagination. Our very conception was imagined. Maybe casual but still imagined. My own conception is directly related to a movie actor, George Raft. When I asked my mother, how is it that a seventeen-year-old white high-school drop-out (as my mother was at that time) meets up with a reservation Indian and conceives me? And she smiled and said, "Jerry, your father looked just like George Raft."

So I must always thank Hollywood as well as my tribal origins and imagination. Momaday was talking about Indians, about Native American Indians, that the worst that can befall us is to go unimagined. And today, we are talking about the imagination of tribal stories, and the power of tribal stories to heal. Stories that enlighten and relieve and relive. Stories that create as they're being told. And stories that overturn the burdens of our human existence. The trickster is one of the most important, one of the most playful, and the most revealing characters of imagination in any literature. A figuration in literature that truly surpasses any other culture's presentation except perhaps for one, and that's the Monkey King, the mind monkey, of traditional folk stories from China. I'd like to think that Naanabozho and the mind monkey of China are first cousins. I brought them so together in a novel entitled *Griever: An American Monkey King in China*.

The trickster arises in imagination and the trickster lives nowhere else but in imagination. We must all have a trickster in the mind if we have any sense of play and imagination about literature. The trickster is a brilliant tribal figure of imagination that has found a new world in written languages. The trickster is personified, as Kimberly Blaeser has pointed out, in many forms, such as animal, spider, bird, avian, arboreal, human, stone, what we would consider in contemporary categories as inanimate and animate. And trickster is also a thought. A thought on the rise. A thought on the fall. A thought of overthrow. A thought left over. The trickster in the oral tradition, however, would overturn the very printed page on which his name has been printed. And certainly the trickster would blur the television screen and trick the reader and the viewer to remember that the real world is imagination, that the real world, the memorable world is one of play, serious play, indeed, but play, and a language game. And the new world is one of performance and creation, rather than a world that is discovered, dependent, and consumed. The new world, the trickster world, doesn't appear on television. The new world, the trickster world, is struggling to find a place on the printed page.

A character in one of my novels said (as if I didn't know this) that the real world is imagination, and all the rest is bad television. Our imagination is real. Our stories are real. We come alive with the trickster in our own imagination, and the rest is bad television. The trickster is not an image on television. The best tribal tricksters are in the best stories shared by people who trust imagination and the pleasures of language games. The very first stories told, the first stories heard, the first imaginative acts and continuous imaginative acts were not consigned to some functional purpose but arose in a burst of enthusiasm and imagination that suited the occasion, that enhances the moment.

Now to be more specific. I'd like to argue for several critical points about the trickster, or what I have come to call trickster discourse. What I mean by that overused word is the engagement in a communal sense of ideas, and meaning, and touch, and imagination. The principal problems that lead to these arguments are: translation from oral stories or sound as a source of reality to the printed page or the visual or sight as the source of reality. I think this is an important consequence in the shift of realities from tribal cultures to contemporary consumer cultures. That tribal cultures, and perhaps many other people today, depend primarily upon sound as a source of reality. The contemporary impact of consumerism has been to shift our sources of reality from sound, which we imagine as we hear, to sight, in a passive consumer culture.

However, the page comes alive with a trickster story in imagination. Surely the trickster is a good story, and as a good story, would be misrepresented on the page, even the exaggeration in a book would be a misrepresentation. Even a trickster reading these books about himself or herself would turn the libraries back into trees and probably talk about sex, wealth, and the wicked breath of greed, and the autumn leaves.

Here are some of my arguments about trickster discourse, but no trickster in heard stories would agree, and there we have a language game. In other words, some tricksters would controvert and overturn everything said or heard in stories. Trickster stories are not liturgies.

Tricksters are real in stories but not in the flesh. Tricksters are not blood or material, but imagination. Tricksters are the kind of thought that raises hope, that heals, that cures, that cannot be traced. The power of a trickster would be diminished, even abolished, by human representations. Humans are not tricksters, but tricksters can be human. Tricksters are not mortal but live forever in imagination. And the trickster is not immortal either. Tricksters liberate the mind, and they do so in a language game. Tricksters do not represent the real or the material. Tricksters are not alive in tribal imagination to prove theories of the social sciences. Tricksters have become anthropologists, but no anthropologist has ever understood a trickster. Tricksters have become anthropologists if only long enough to overturn their theories and turn them into cold shit. But tricksters are not moral or functional. Tricksters are not artifacts. Tricksters never prove culture or the absence of culture. Tricksters do not prove the values that we live by, nor do they prove or demonstrate the responses to domination by colonial democracies. Tricksters are not consumables. Tricksters are not breakfast cereal. Tricksters are ethereal. Tricksters only exist in a comic sense between two people who take pleasure in a language game and imagination, a noetic liberation of the mind. The trickster must represent imagination as the real, nothing more than that. Nothing more than that could ever be healing. What we consume is not the best source of healing energies. The only way an anthropologist can understand a trickster is to know that tricksters are never possessed by understanding. Tricksters prevailed in imagination, but not in consumable facts or definitions. The trickster prevails in what the social sciences lack. Tricksters prevail and heal in what the social sciences lack, lack the most of, imagination. Imagination is dangerous in the social sciences. It can bring a serious dissertation and promotion with tenure to a grim terminal conclusion. The trickster could be compassionate on the printed page—*could* be compassionate. I argue that the trickster must appear, at least in the beginning scene, as compassionate. There is however, a literary preoccupation with the confidence man in American literature. (And there aren't many confidence women, but confidence men.) I think one reason the trickster has disappeared from American literary imagination is because literature has been consumed. And the trickster has been consumed by the social sciences, by way of definitions and functional descriptions. I need only refer you to Paul Radin's outstanding work on the trickster which is nevertheless flawed because he acts in a superior, narrative manner. He said the tribes who told these stories believed in this trickster as a superhuman being, godlike. Surely, in any story a trickster would overturn his godliness and superhumanness.

Even more odious is the work of Victor Barnouw, who translated, interpreted, and published a book on the Wisconsin Chippewa trickster stories. Barnouw did what many social scientists have done, he imposed theories in order to interpret a free spirit, a liberation of the mind. He imposed theories that brought imagination to its knees by way of the passive verb. Barnouw imposed psychoanalytic theory of the most despicable kind in the form of the Rorschach Test, if you can believe it. And to one of the most generous, liberating healers, who trusted this man and who told him some of the most wonderful, playful stories, to whom Barnouw should have felt blessed, graced, and forever beholden, Barnouw gave a Rorschach Test, and a Thematic Apperception Test, and then he interpreted for us as readers the meaning of these stories based on these tests. This generous healer who shared his stories with this anthropologist was in Barnouw's terms "sexually repressed," and "sexually undeveloped," and "inhibited." Alas, the story teller was diminished and the anthropologist was promoted.

Trickster is understandable in the comic mode of literary theory.

And to just touch on the values of comic interpretations of literature—they're communal, they make for an experience where chance, unknown factors, and spontaneity, give rise to significant meaning in life. But comic situations are not possible without a group, without a communal experience. To do otherwise comes close to psychopathology or schizophrenia, to walk around telling your own stories and laughing at yourself. That would be the tragic mode, which is the primary literary interpretation that has been used to interpret almost all of Native American culture, literature, and song. The tragic mode. It celebrates individualism. It celebrates the pursuit of causes and moral issues greater than life itself. The tragic celebrates the touch of the gods, good or bad, at least in classical literature. And in the Renaissance and Enlightenment, the mode shifted to the feudal lords: how sad and tragic that they lost their power. And in contemporary time we derive certain pleasures from the variations on the tragic mode in the anti-tragic character who appears in films, let's say, and in some novels. Much like us, this tragic character suffers a lot of problems with the bureaucracy, with families, and police, the post office, et cetera. And his paranoid responses are all true. And he never rises above them, just muddles along in good humor by himself, somewhat isolated, nobody understands, and ends up either fired or quitting his job, and surfing for ten years in California. That's been an acceptable theme as a tragic interpretation of life. Unfortunately, the tragic mode of interpretation has been imposed on almost all interpretations of Native American experience, culture, literature, and especially the trickster stories. The individual has been celebrated at the expense of clearly present communal dynamic cultures. I need only refer you to the photographs of Edward Curtis to prove this point in the visual arts, to point out that almost all of his photographs celebrate the stoical portraiture of the individual against the wilderness and the gods. Against the wilderness of his own soul. Rarely, you can count on one hand the photographs that show any community. Curtis seldom pictured Indians at work. Now, some of this is explained, of course, because Curtis first started his work when exposure times were a minute to three minutes on a glass plate. But even so, within his brilliant career as a photographer, photography advanced to a point where he wouldn't have had to do that, but he continued to celebrate the stoical, isolated individual, the tragic hero who lost his culture, lost his race, and stands against a withered landscape as evidence of the vanishing race.

The trickster above all is a measure indeed of our own imagination. And in that sense the trickster could be an endangered figuration, an endangered metaphor, an endangered sign of a healing practice in tribal cultures, even in book form. In a very informative book by Richard Kearney, entitled *The Wake of Imagination*, he writes that it's virtually impossible today to contemplate a so-called "natural setting" without some consumerist media image lurking in the back of one's mind. "The psychic world," he writes, "is as colonized as the physical world by the whole image industry" of a consumer culture. Trickster could be an endangered figuration in this consumer culture. "The culture of the Book is being replaced," he writes, "by a culture of the Image. Some even claim we are entering an era when reading may become an anachronism. Little more than a nostalgic luxury."

"The contemporary eye is no longer innocent. What we see is almost invariably informed by pre-fabricated images. There is, of course, a fundamental difference between the image of today and of former times: now the image *precedes* the reality." We consume the image as experience before it's real. We have no experience before the consumption of the image. The image *precedes* the reality it is supposed to represent. Or to put it another way, reality has become a pale reflection of the image."[2]

Wily Coyote, the cartoon, is wonderful and entertaining, but it's also an image that's being consumed, and the coyote figure is probably close to being one of the great southwestern *kitsch* items of contemporary experience. It's symbolic on tee-shirts, carved wooden coyotes howling at the moon, in pastel pinks, and ceramics, and I was just told that we must stop on our way home in Kansas City at the Coyote Restaurant. Where they serve, no doubt, edible menus. Where the pictures are good and nutritious, and you only order a couple of picture cards and eat on the road.

One of the greatest paradoxes of contemporary culture is that at the time when the image reigns supreme the very notion of a creative human imagination seems to be under mounting threat. According to Richard Kearney, the "imminent demise of imagination is clearly a postmodern obsession. Postmodernism undermines the modernist belief in the image as an *authentic* expression. The typical postmodern image is one which displays its own artificiality, its own pseudo-status, its own representational depthlessness."[3]

I forgot to tell you what I was going to do. I was going to be seriously playful in this first part, and then playfully serious in the second part. I am going to read a short first chapter from a new novel, *The Heirs of Columbus*, a contribution to the 500-year kitschy celebration of the pseudo-discoverer of the route to the Indies. And that doesn't have anything to do with me, I'm only reporting the truth, and the truth is Christopher Columbus was a Mayan Indian. You laugh, Jesus Christ was Mayan, too, and I'm looking into the possibility that Moses and other distinguished religious leaders, and those who have a part in the current hierarchy of the Vatican, may indeed have the signature of survivance from the great explorers of Mayan civilization. The premise is not too hard to accept because there have been a number of diffusion theories suggesting that in fact Indians went the other way. There's not one scrap of evidence to support the so-called scientific deduction that Indians crossed the Bering Strait. And even if there were some evidence, it probably wouldn't be convincing enough to tell us which way. Which is a point that a character in my film *Harold of Orange* tells with pleasure. "Which way?" And the white guy says, "Whattaya mean, which way?" He said, "I mean which way, from here to there or there to here?" And there have been a number of ideas and theories and pretty wonderful, imaginative, wacky propositions that the Mayan sailed east and settled in the Mediterranean and North Africa and had something to do with teaching the Egyptians how to do their business.

My story starts, or is based on, this potential. That Mayans did travel many places, and that now their heirs live in northern Minnesota. And this is proven by the fact that a certain number of people who are Chippewa and who say they are the heirs of Christopher Columbus in spite of all the snickering that goes on about this, and derision, that an Indian mixed-blood from Minnesota should claim that he's related to Christopher Columbus. You can imagine the suffering they've gone through. In spite of that they can prove that they are heirs of Christopher Columbus because they have scientifically established a unique genetic signature, a code that's only inherited by women and has been passed through Columbus from Mayans who settled in the Old World, and Columbus brought it back to the New World, and that was part of his inspiration. His dedication to get here was a kind of mystery. He was driven by his blood to return to his homeland. And on the way he ran into a Chippewa woman who also was an heir, who had the signature of survivance, and you'll see what happens.

The heirs of Christopher Columbus are serious over their names and resurrections. The heirs come together at the Stone Tavern in the autumn to remember the best stories about their strain and estate, and their genetic signature that heals the obvious blunders in the natural world. This Stone Tavern is a wonderous circle of warm trickster stones. And it's been located for more than a hundred generations near the headwaters of the Mississippi River. The Anishinaabe, the woodland tribe that founded this obscure Stone Tavern—the oldest tavern in the New World, might I add—remember that the trickster who created the world had a brother who was a stone, a bear stone, a human stone, a shaman stone, a stone. The stones are warm at the tavern, and in the winter that sacred circle near the headwaters is a haven for birds and animals and stories of liberation.

Stone Columbus heard the summer in the spring once more on the occasion of his third resurrection (I read that recently and said erection instead of resurrection.) That season the rush of aspen touched him as a child on his first return from a furnace. He came back a second time in the arms of the notorious Ice Woman, and then he drowned in his bingo caravel and heard the push of bears.

None of these stories would be true if he had not inherited the surname and the signature of survivance from the great Admiral of the Ocean Sea.

The heirs of Columbus celebrate the quintessence of their inheritance every autumn. The heirs told their stories about creation, the bear codex, and handtalkers, and the Ice Woman, and moccasin games. Stories about the panic hole tricksters, and especially stories about the bingo caravel, and third death and resurrection of the sovereign mariner Stone Columbus. (They had pull tabs there, too.)

Christopher Columbus appeared in the dreams of these heirs. The stories that were told at the headwaters were ceremonies, remembrance in the blood. Because their bear codex, the last record of their signature and blood histories, had been lost at sea, and they must remember the creation in their own telling. None others on the reservation were visited in dreams or stories by the great explorer. Rather, those who revealed their dreams in his name were shunned. Shunned for a while, until the caravels turned a fortune on sovereign bingo. And then they were popular.

Stone Columbus was heartened by his esoteric genetic signatures, and the stories in his blood. He was a crossblood and his spiritual distance from the tribe seemed natural at first. To be sure, the personal miseries and public troubles from white men over the centuries were blamed on the estranged stories that the heirs told in the Stone Tavern. The heirs were burdened with withering ironies of those who had never beheld these wonderful resurrections.

The *Santa Maria* Casino, that decorated bingo flagship, was anchored on the international border near Big Island in Lake of the Woods. The caravel was an enormous barge that had been decked for games of chance on the high seas of the woodland. The *Nina* was a restaurant, and the *Pinta* a tax-free smokeshop. These three caravels were anchored and moored in Lake of the Woods. The *Santa Maria* was christened and launched as soon as the ice broke in the spring. Stone built a cantilevered stern-castle and a cabin that overlooked the spacious casino. So that on one level he heard the seasons and on the lower level he watched the players in the lounge.

The other caravels were fitted and christened by early summer in time for the tourists and their search for gold and tribal adventures.

The Fourth of July, however, that year was not a celebration of tribal independence. Stone was arrested and detained on warrants that charged him with violations of state tax and gambling laws. And the caravels were towed to a public dock. The next morning, however, a federal judge reversed the state court order. She'd agreed to review the issues of tribal sovereignty. Our tribal mariner of chance was back at sea, anchored once more to his imagined border. In the first two summers on the water he made a fortune on games, and waited for the court to rule on his right to operate a casino as a new reservation moored to an anchor. Law enforcement agencies from both nations circled the caravel every day. They copied boat and airplane numbers. They estimated the tax-free cash flow of the gamblers. And they anticipated daily the court decision that would sink this savage *Santa Maria* Casino.

Robin Lord, the federal judge (no relation to Miles Lord), ruled in favor of the unusual casino, and sanctioned this reservation on an anchor. She so admired the imagination and certitude of the founder that she announced the court decision from the sterncastle of the *Santa Maria* on Columbus Day. She said, over a loudspeaker, "The federal court finds in favor of Stone Columbus. The notion of tribal sovereignty is not tied just to the earth. Sovereignty is neither fence nor feathers. The very essence of sovereignty is tribal, communal, and spiritual. An idea that is more than metes and bounds and treaties. The court vacated the claims of the state and ruled that an anchor and caravel are as much tribal connections to sovereignty as a homestead, mineral rights, or even the sacred cedar."

"The *Santa Maria* and other caravels are limited sovereign states at sea. The first maritime reservations in international waters," said the judge. "Moreover," she said, the "defendant was wise to drop his anchors on the border, knowing as he must that future appeals and other remedies could reach the International Court of Justice in the Hague."

The sovereign casino was a natural sensation that summer. Net-

work television reported on "the tribe that was lost no more." And
on the genetic theories of the crossblood founder of the new casino
tribes, who traced his descent to the great adventurer Christopher
Columbus.

Stone posed on television with Felipa Flowers, the gorgeous trickster poacher who lived with him on the caravel. But he would never
speak to a camera as I'm doing. He agreed, however, to be heard on
national talk-show radio. "Radio is real, television is not," he said.
His grandparents listened to talk radio late at night on the reservation. The arguments he heard as a child stimulated his imagination,
his sense of adventure in stories. Stone was heard by millions of
people late at night on radio that wild summer. The cross-blood of
the northern air told stories about the Stone Tavern, his resurrections, and the genetic signatures of the heirs that would heal the
nation. He spoke from the bridge of his caravel. Thousands of people circled the casino in canoes, and float planes from the cities. The
gamblers were white. Most were on vacation. They were urban ad-
venturers who would lose at bingo and slot machines on a moored
reservation.

"Admiral White is on the air, your late-night radio host on CARP
radio." The radio was heard in four directions from the enormous
loudspeakers on the masts.

"Stone is back to answer your questions and mine. Here we go
once more with the truth in the dark. So how do you expect our
listeners to buy those stories that your brother is a stone, a common
rock?"

"Stone is my name, not my brother. And we are not common,"
said Stone. His voice was a primal sound that boomed over the
black water. "The stone is my totem, my stories, there are stones in
my tribal families, and the brother of the first trickster who created
the earth was a stone."

"Really, but how can you be a stone, a real stone, and be talking
on radio?" she asked, and then paused for a commercial. The talks
from the casino two or three nights a week had attracted new listeners and eager advertisers.

"Stones hold our tribal origins and our worlds in silence in the

same way that we listen in stories and hold our past in memories,"
said Stone.

"Stone, listen, our listeners know that you were born on a reservation, and we understand how proud you are to be an Indian, so
can you claim to be a direct descendent of a stone and Christopher
Columbus?"

"Columbus was Maya," said Stone.

"You must be stoned," she said. Her voice bounced on the water
and the boats rocked with laughter near the casino.

"Really you must be stoned on that reservation boat, Columbus
was Italian not a Mayan Indian."

"The Maya brought civilization to the savages of the Old World,
and the rest is natural," said Stone. "Columbus carried the tribal
genes back to the New World, back to the Great River. He was an
adventurer in the blood, and he returned to his homeland."

"His homeland? Now wait a minute, this is serious radio, Stone."

"My stories are always serious," he said.

Stone posed on the bridge at the *Santa Maria*. The mast was decorated with spiritcatchers that held wild beads of light from the boats
on the lake. Felipa touched him, the wonderous trickster at sea in a
scarlet tunic.

"Mayan genes. Give me a break," said the admiral.

"The truth is in genes. We are the tribal heirs of the great explorer
who was here at the headwaters searching for gold and tribal
women. And he's here in our blood and stories now."

"So what did he find then?" asked the admiral on CARP radio.
"Samana, the golden tribal woman, is what he found."

"Now we get the real story."

"Samana is a handtalker, a golden woman of the islands and sister
to the fish, and she caught his eye and she set that adventurer free on
October 28, 1492, on the island now named Cuba," he said, and
smiled over the dates and names.

Felipa danced on the deck that warm night. She was touched by
the memories of his stories, the sound of creation, and she sensed

the end of the heartsore stories of a broken civilization. She sensed the end of loneliness.

"Stone, wait a minute, you leaped from stones to genes to gold-fish to dates and places and back again, so take your time now, spell it out in your own words to our listeners," said Admiral White.

"October 29, 1492, at Rio de la Luna. . . ."

"You changed the date."

"Columbus is on the move," said Stone.

"This is a good time for a commercial," said the radio admiral.

Stone disconnected the microphone and the power to the loud-speakers. The moon was a wicked sliver in the west. On the water the moon was shredded on the breeze. Felipa undressed and dove into the black water. Stone followed and they swam to the island and made love on a granite boulder. The mosquitoes sounded in their heat. They could hear the bears. The breath of bears. Later a cool wind touched them. The Ice Woman lived in a cave on the other side of the island.

"The Ice Woman saved me once," he said, on the cool granite. "I crashed through the thin ice. The paper ice that teased me to cross in the spring and sank deeper and deeper in the cold water. I could see the hole in the ice above me, and the veins on the underside of the ice, but my arms were numbed, my vision blurred, and the last breath of cold water was ecstatic. The Ice Woman brought me back, my second resurrection."

The *Santa Maria* Casino paid high stakes to hundreds of winners, and earned millions besides. And the tax-free market caravel was a second gold-mine. Stone earned more than a million dollars a sea-son, and there were four summers in the name of the great explorer. Even the restaurant caravel turned a profit on pretentious bad taste—a "commodities menu" of fry-bread, oatmeal, macaroni, and glorified wild rice.

Stone was the proud mariner of a naval reservation in the New World. He heard the seasons turn from the bridge of the *Santa Maria*. He heard the summer in the spring, and discovered gold in the name of his blood and survivance. Then one night in a thunderstorm, at the crowning point of his casino glories, the caravels were cracked by lightening. Felipa was on shore and survived the storm. The few gamblers in the casino were able to abandon the caravels and rode the storm in their own boats. The spiritcatchers on the mast burned, and the blue medicine poles were overturned and crashed into the casino. The *Santa Maria* lost her anchor and moorings as a sovereign casino. She bashed on a granite reef. The beam groaned, and the caravel sank near the island. The sudden end of a reservation. The great explorer discovered gold and then drowned in his sacred tunic. He washed ashore, a rich man with thousands of bingo cards. Stone was broken and lost on the cold granite. His black hair was mussed with weeds and wild tinsel. The bears pushed the seasons down to the shore at dawn and pawed the remains of the caravels, the spiritcatchers, macaroni, polyurethane, lost at sea in the last thunderstorm of the season.

Samana, the crossblood black bear and lonesome handtalker on the island hauled the mariner to a granite boulder. She teased his ears with her nose and blew on his eyes and mouth. When she blew harder, the other bears danced on the mount. Rose was a shaman. Samana was a shaman. As her mother was a bear and her touch would heal the air with stories in the blood. Samana touched his head and the bears pushed him back from death with a blue radiance. The stones were warmed on the shore. He was a handtalker in the maw, she was his heart and memories. She teased his third resurrection in the stone.

GERALD VIZENOR, former journalist for the *Minneapolis Tribune,* is Professor of Native American Literature at the University of California, Berkeley. He has published many books about Native American experience, including five novels. His most recent books are *Manifest Manners,* a collection of essays, and *Shadow Distance: A Gerald Vizenor Reader.*

Notes

1. N. Scott Momaday, "The Man Made of Words," in *Indian Voices: First Convocation of American Indian Scholars* (San Francisco: Indian Historian Press, 1970), p. 55.

2. Richard Kearney, *The Wake of Imagination* (Minneapolis: University of Minnesota Press, 1988), 1, 2.

3. Kearney, 3.

Suggestions for Further Reading

Radin, Paul. *The Trickster: A Study in American Indian Mythology.* New York: Greenwood Press, 1969; New York: Schocken, 1987.

Vizenor, Gerald. *Bearheart: The Heirship Chronicles.* Minneapolis: University of Minnesota Press, 1990.

Vizenor, Gerald R. *Crossbloods: Bone Courts, Bingo, and Other Reports.* Minneapolis: University of Minnesota Press, 1990.

Vizenor, Gerald R. *Dead Voices: Natural Agonies in the New World.* Norman: University of Oklahoma Press, 1992.

Vizenor, Gerald. *Earthdivers: Tribal Narratives on Mixed Descent.* Minneapolis: University of Minnesota Press, 1981.

Vizenor, Gerald R. *Greiver, An American Monkey King in China: A Novel.* New York: Fiction Collective, 1987.

Vizenor, Gerald R. *The Heirs of Columbus.* Middletown, CT: Wesleyan University Press; Hanover, NH: University Press of New England, 1991.

Vizenor, Gerald R. *Interior Landscapes: Autobiographical Myths and Metaphors.* Minneapolis: University of Minnesota Press, 1990.

Vizenor, Gerald R. *Landfill Meditations: Crossblood Stories.* Hanover, NH: Wesleyan University Press, 1991.

Vizenor, Gerald R. *Narrative Chance: Postmodern Discourse on Native American Indian Literatures.* Albuquerque: University of New Mexico Press, 1989; Norman: University of Oklahoma Press, 1993.

Vizenor, Gerald R. *The People Named the Chippewa: Narrative Histories.* Minneapolis: University of Minnesota Press, 1984.

Vizenor, Gerald R. *Summer in the Spring: Anishinaabe Lyric Poems and Stories.* Norman: University of Oklahoma Press, 1993.

Vizenor, Gerald R. *Touchwood: A Collection of Ojibway Prose.* St. Paul, MN: New Rivers Press, 1987.

Vizenor, Gerald R. *Trickster of Liberty: Tribal Heirs to a Wild Baronage.* Minneapolis: University of Minnesota Press, 1988.

Vizenor, Gerald. *Wordarrows: Indians and Whites in the New Fur Trade.* Minneapolis: University of Minnesota Press, 1978.

Why Treaties?

Frederick E. Hoxie

D'Arcy McNickle Center for the
History of the American Indian,
Newberry Library

I t has become a spring ritual. Members of Ojibwa communities in northern Wisconsin set out to fish in the barely ice-free waters of the region's lakes. They do this because treaties their ancestors negotiated with the United States 150 years ago stipulated that they could continue to harvest resources at their customary hunting and fishing sites even though they would live on circumscribed lands called reservations. When they arrive at public boat landings, the Indians are met by groups of angry whites who picket the lake shore, chant slogans and protest to anyone within earshot that an old treaty should not excuse people from following the state fish and game laws. As the drama unfolds, other players appear: local politicians (both Indian and white), officials of the Department of Natural Resources, support groups to bolster the fishing parties or to augment the lakeside pickets, and—the final validation—television crews from Milwaukee, Chicago, and New York.

Indian leaders state their case simply and eloquently. Treaties (in this case agreements signed in

1837, 1842, and 1854) are "the supreme law of the land." Indians have a superior right to fish because of those treaties. Now that federal courts have upheld their claims, protecting Indian fishing rights is purely a matter of law enforcement.

The opposition, fueled by economic worries (the area is heavily dependent on tourism) and racial hatred, is equally forthright. The executive director of the Wisconsin Counties Association argues that "the exercise of treaty rights is not in tune with contemporary society."[1] Assisted by other groups with names like Stop Treaty Abuse and the Citizens Equal Rights Alliance, the Counties Association points out that times have changed: tribal economies are no longer reliant on fishing as they were in the nineteenth century, and tribal communities contain many people of mixed ancestry. They argue that the treaties were written for another era, and that it is time to "modernize" the old agreements.

Luckily—miraculously, really—no one has been killed in these face-offs, which have reached their peak each April. They are frightening events which bring to mind the school desegregation crisis in Boston in the 1970s, the open housing marches in Chicago in the 1960s, and earlier confrontations between federal authority and state officials in the Deep South. And, as with these other cases involving African Americans, the well-publicized confrontations in Wisconsin have been repeated in a variety of settings across the United States. The state of Washington engaged an array of tribes in a decades-long struggle over salmon runs in Puget Sound. There, as in Wisconsin, when federal courts upheld a nineteenth-century treaty guarantee, state officials and local fishing interests fought it, and antagonists reached an uneasy peace after years of strife. The state of Wyoming is currently obsessed with another sacred western resource—water—which treaties granted the Indians of the Wind River Reservation but which non-Indian farmers have grown accustomed to using. In Montana, where the issue is coal, the sides are a little different: Indians want to mine it and whites have opposed them on environmental grounds. The tribes have cited their treaties to defend their right to exploit the resource.

In each of these cases—and in dozens of others around the

country—Indians and their opponents have quarreled over the idea that tribal members have special prerogatives under American law. Native Americans claim that their property is in some way sovereign. It is, to use the dictionary equivalents of sovereign, "supreme, paramount, independent." Tribal areas, they argue, resemble national states. The mark of this sovereignty, this national existence, is the treaty—the 370-odd documents which were negotiated, signed, and approved by authorized commissioners and representatives from particular tribes and subsequently ratified by the U.S. Senate.

The existence of nearly four hundred tribes raises a series of difficult historical questions. First, why did the United States choose this form of relationship with the indigenous peoples of North America? The Canadian government negotiated vastly fewer treaties with that country's Indians, and it made clear throughout the process that all sovereignty resided with the central government. (The Canadian government really viewed the treaties as land sales. Officials there still refer to their treaties as "treaties and surrenders.") Mexico and the other Latin American countries have no treaties with tribal groups. The government of New Zealand signed one treaty with Maori leaders; the Australians signed none with native peoples. Thus, Americans are unique in both the number of treaties they negotiated and the sense of sovereignty they embody.

Second, why did the U.S. make so many treaties? Assuming some practical reason for treaty-making in the first days of the republic, why did the American government maintain the practice after the balance of power had shifted so strongly in its favor? Again, the New Zealanders signed one treaty in 1840 and then tried to forget about it. Why didn't we do the same?

Third, why have Americans followed these treaties? It is remarkable that a society of people who can't remember Jimmy Carter would treat these obscure documents with such reverence. We have forgotten Sunday closing laws, and we ignore the doctrine of state's rights, so why do we remember Indian treaties?

Finally, how can we reconcile the history of the constitution with the persistence of treaty-making? Generalizations are dangerous, but it seems to me that constitutional history is largely the story of the expansion of individual liberty, not only in the guarantees of the Bill of Rights, but in the extension of citizenship to ex-slaves, women, and eighteen-year-olds. Treaty opponents argue that treaty rights privilege one group over another and undermine the notion of equal citizenship. What is the response to that? How are special treaty rights constitutional? In today's political labels, are they entitlements, racially-based affirmative action, or compensatory legislation?

Each of these questions deserves an essay in itself. I will try to respond to each of them, but the first is fundamental. Let me try to answer that one fully, and then use the remaining time to address the other three briefly.

Why treaties? To answer this question we need to go back to the first days of the American government. The United States Senate was called to order as prescribed by the newly-ratified constitution on March 4, 1789. Because a number of members were still enroute to the capital city of New York, that maiden event was unremarkable: the group lacked a quorum and adjourned. It did not achieve a quorum for a month. Once the members were present, however, the Senate went to work ratifying the election of the President, establishing the new government's various departments, and setting up its committee system. In the midst of its first month's work—even before cabinet officers were confirmed or the judiciary organized—President Washington sent his first executive message to the Senate.

The President's first message was a report from Secretary of War Henry Knox which contained two agreements signed by representatives of the United States and "certain northern and northwestern tribes" at Fort Harmar on the Muskingum River in Ohio (an area ceded by the British in 1783 but not yet formally organized into a state or federal territory). Knox and Washington recommended that the Senate consent to these agreements under the procedure for the ratification of treaties in the new constitution. In effect, they were asking Congress to equate Indian treaties with other international agreements.

Everyone involved realized that they were making a fundamental decision. The constitution did not prescribe treatymaking as the basis for Indian-white contact. The new document stated only that Congress would have the power to "regulate commerce with foreign nations, and among the several states, and with the Indian tribes." It did not indicate the form this regulation would take. In the section on the powers of the President, it said he could "make treaties," but it did not say with whom.

The ambiguity was deepened by the phrase "Indians not taxed" which appeared in Article I in reference to the apportionment of seats in the House of Representatives. "Indians not taxed" were not counted for purposes of allocating representation. This could mean that Indians were to be excluded from the government or it could mean that they were to be included, but only after they became dues-paying members of the new American society.

Washington could have recommended that the Harmar agreements be approved by resolution, or he could have avoided the documents altogether and simply requested an appropriation to fulfill the obligations contained in them. Congress would probably have gone along with him and there never would have been any treaties. Why did he want treaties?

First, there were practical considerations. The Indians were numerous, the British were still very much in evidence in the Great Lakes country (they still occupied posts), the Spanish were firmly settled in their two-hundred-year old settlements in Florida, and the American government was broke. While they met in the spring of 1789, Daniel Shays was about to be pardoned for leading the first American tax revolt, and as military men Washington and Knox knew how expensive Indian wars could be. They were not eager to test the will of eastern tax-payers to subsidize the expansion of western settlements. Given this reality, Knox predicted that the alternative to formal treaties was disaster. He wrote in his report to the Senate:

In case no treaty should be held, the events which are rising in rapid succession on the frontiers, must be suffered to take their own course. Their progress and issue will deeply injure, if not utterly destroy, the interests and government of the United States in the Western Territory.[2]

Second, the administration urged ratification of the treaties in order to prevent individual states from acting on their own. Ironically, Indian treaties were originally a badge of sovereignty for the national government (Indians didn't need sovereignty at that time!). Elevating relations with Indians to the level of treaty-making would preclude the possibility of separate state agreements with tribes. If Indians held federal treaties (always described as "the supreme law of the land"), state agreements would clearly be inferior and unattractive. Formal treaties would pre-empt the state and guarantee the federal government exclusive jurisdiction over Indian affairs.

Washington made this point in August of 1789 while the Harmar agreements still awaited action; the President took the unprecedented step of sitting down with the Senate to discuss conflicts between the Creek Indians and the state of Georgia. Led by a brilliant mixed-blood commander named Alexander McGillivray and supplied by the Spanish at Pensacola, the Creeks in 1787 and 1788 had expelled white intruders on their land and threatened to roll back Georgia's borders. In his discussions with the Senate, the President proceeded delicately. He wanted to calm the fears of the Georgians, but he also wanted to prevent the state's "hawks" from launching a unilateral attack on the Creeks. The attack would undoubtedly draw the United States into war with the Indians and their Spanish sponsors, with a potentially chaotic outcome. He advised the senators that conciliating "the powerful tribes of Indians in the southern district . . . and [attaching] them firmly to the United States, may be regarded as highly worthy of the serious attention of the government."[3]

The President and the Senate decided to dispatch federal commissioners to Georgia to negotiate a treaty with the Creeks. One more ticklish question remained. What if the Creeks would not negotiate? Should the commissioners deliver an ultimatum to Mc-Gillivray? Washington's response was clear: no.

The President was wise to make this clear, for as it happened, the negotiations in Georgia proved fruitless. When that became evident, Washington invited McGillivray to New York. In the summer of 1790 the Creek leader and his lieutenants arrived in the American capital and signed a treaty which provided, among other things, for McGillivray's appointment to the rank of brigadier general in the American army (at $1200 a year), and allowed the tribe to import $60,000 per year in trade goods duty-free. Alexander McGillivray apparently believed the dictum: be sovereign, act sovereign.

With the Creek discussions behind him, Washington pressed the Senate to act on Knox's May report. The Senate's new Indian affairs committee opposed treating the agreements as treaties, but the President insisted. He sent another special message to the upper house on September 17, expanding on his earlier arguments:

> It is said to be the general understanding and practice of nations, as a check on the mistakes and indiscretions of Ministers or Commissioners, not to consider any treaty negotiated and signed by such officers as final and conclusive until ratified by the sovereign or government from whom they derive their powers: this practice has been adopted by the United States respecting their treaties with European Nations; and I am inclined to think it would be advisable to observe it in the conduct of our treaties with the Indians: for tho such treaties, being on their part made by their chiefs or rulers, need not be ratified by them, yet being formed on our part by the agency of subordinate officers, it seems to be both prudent and reasonable that their acts should not be binding on the nation until approved and ratified by and settled, so that our national proceedings in this respect may become uniform, and directed by fixed and stable principles.[4]

Washington seems to be discussing irresponsible treaty commissioners, but the real message here is that treaties would be *binding on the nation* and therefore would give the national government a way to hold the states to *uniform, fixed,* and *stable principles.* On September 22, 1789, the Senate decided to ratify the Fort Harmar treaties, thereby establishing the practice of formal treaty-making as the basis for United States Indian policy.

A third reason for this decision should be mentioned. I have stressed practical considerations because Washington by nature was a practical man and because he had no sympathy for Indian people (he referred to them as "wolves"). But there was the ideological reason: treaties seemed the fairest, most just way for a new nation to proceed, especially a nation which claimed to represent justice and liberty. Frankly, this ideological consideration does not appear paramount in the American leaders' minds in 1789, but it was present. Knox said it best. "It is presumable," he noted in his report to the Senate, "that a nation solicitous of establishing its character on the broad basis of justice, would not only hesitate at, but reject, every proposition to benefit itself by the injury of any neighboring community, however contemptible and weak it might be. . . ."

The decision to deal with Indians by treaty was not taken lightly or innocently. The question of ratification forced the young American government to address the significance of its commitments to the tribes and to define the federal government's role in making and maintaining those commitments. By taking the treaty route, Washington and the Senate made clear that Indian affairs would be primarily a federal concern. Associating Indian affairs with federal power would privilege national concerns over local ones and create the opportunity to link national ideology and the treatment of native people. As Knox wrote, to reject treaty relations would "be a gross violation of the fundamental laws of nature and of that distributive justice which is the glory of a nation."[5]

We can answer the question of why there were treaties for 1789, but one other aspect of the story remains unexplained: Where did those Fort Harmar agreements come from? The first senate discussed the issue of treaties seriously, but their debate did not take place in a vacuum. In fact, treaties were central to the European presence in the Americas. From the time of Columbus, questions of ownership, sovereignty, and legitimacy stalked the nations who came here and colored their relations both with each other and with the continent's native people. Treaties—or formal agreements between the leaders of the parties involved—were the principal means of resolving these questions of sovereignty and legitimacy.

Pope Alexander VI's Bull of May 4, 1493, issued less than six months after Columbus's return to Spain, was the first such agreement. Formulated at the request of King Ferdinand and Queen Isabella, the document noted that the monarch had sent the Italian explorer to "discover certain islands and mainlands" so as to bring their residents "to the worship of our redeemer and the profession of the Catholic faith." Having succeeded in "discovering" such lands the Pope declared that Ferdinand and Isabella had proposed "to bring under their sway the said mainlands and islands." Acting on their request the Pope thus declared:

> we . . . out of our own sole largess and certain knowledge and out of the fullness of our apostolic power . . . which we hold on earth, do . . . give grant and assign to you and your heirs and successors . . . forever, . . . all islands and mainlands found and to be found, discovered and to be discovered towards the west and [south of a line] one hundred leagues towards the west and south . . . [of] the Azores . . . .[6]

The Pope went on to exempt any Christian princes who might live in the unknown lands from his order and to promise excommunication and "the wrath of Almighty God" to all who contravened his will. It was as close to a deed as a European monarch could obtain.

The king of France is supposed to have reacted to Alexander's grand bequest by asking, "Where is Adam's will?" The Protestant Reformation no doubt brought forth even nastier comments, but the legacy of this legalistic turn remained. The Spanish organized their empire as an extension of their European kingdom. With viceroys and governors at work in the New World, they could maintain the idea that their empire's borders were the same as the carefully marked borders in Europe. While this imperial model eliminated the need to treat formally with the Indians, it did suggest that any friction between the Spanish and their imperial rivals in the New World would take the form of conflicts between nation-states.

When the conflicts in Europe became contests between Catholic and Protestant states, this condition, too, was projected into the New World. Enemy states would challenge the legitimacy of each other's government as well as a particular disputed border. Thus, imperial rivalries in North America—where the competition between the major powers was greatest—began to involve more than who placed a marker where and who sailed up which river first. Claims to the New World came to involve the nature of European rule.

In the vague mid-Atlantic region of "Virginia," for example, it was not important to the British that the Spanish had landed Jesuits in Chesapeake Bay in the 1570, or that Cartier had sailed along the New England coast in the 1530s. The English were unwilling simply to submit to Spanish and French claims. In addition to claims of first arrival, the English, Dutch, and others began to argue that they were *legitimate* rulers of the new lands because they actually settled them and "planted" colonies there. Roanoke, Jamestown, and Plymouth were British responses to the Papal Bull.

Out of such imperial rivalries grew a series of rules which became the basis for international law. One of these new rules was the notion of adverse possession. Those who use the land own it, regardless of claims from on high. In a sense, Jamestown was an extended adverse possession claim against Spain. Writing in 1688, the German legal theorist Samuel von Pufendorf defined the concept this way: "Whoever has continued the possession of a thing for the period prescribed by law . . . has something added to him which he has thus far lacked."[7] By possessing territory, in the European sense, one could become the sovereign over it.

Adverse possession was a two-edged sword. It allowed European powers to settle on and claim ownership of native lands, and it was therefore another instrument of imperialism. But it also encouraged Europeans to negotiate agreements with Indians who "possessed" their lands and therefore might have the power to recognize European rule. By accepting a new monarch, tribes were in effect conveying sovereignty to him or her. Again, to return to James-town, the English were intent on crowning the local Indian leader—Powhatan—"king" of the Indians as a recognition of his leadership under their rule.

But by accepting nominal European control, Native Americans were also clothing their own possessions in the mantle of European international law. This mantle did not interest Powhatan—they had to lean on his shoulders to crown him—but as rivalries intensi-fied in the eighteenth century and native people became more de-pendent on Europeans for weapons and tools, the relationship be-tween tribal leaders and European crowns became more appealing. Soon Indian leaders welcomed the treaty council as a ceremony of trade and friendship. They came to value their alliances with Euro-peans as instruments that brought them both security and wealth. That the actions were interpreted among Europeans as acts of sur-render did not interest them at this juncture.

The relationship of the Iroquois and the English in the eighteenth century provides the most instructive example of mutual reinforce-ment. The English grew increasingly dependent on the Mohawks and, through them, the entire Iroquois council to provide assistance against the French and access to the Great Lakes fur trade. For their part, the Iroquois relied on the English to supply them with trade goods and to reward their leaders. The mark of the power of that alliance was, first, the terror with which American leaders contem-plated the Iroquois alliance with Great Britain in the American Revolution, and, second, the wholesale transfer of the Iroquois un-der the leadership of the Mohawk Joseph Brant to the Grand River in Ontario after the war.

The treaties that the Continental Congress and the Confedera-tion government negotiated with Indian groups prior to 1789 were extensions of colonial practice. They were intended to win the loy-alty of the groups involved (and therefore to make some claim to be sovereigns over them), and they were intended to secure military alliances for the purpose of defending themselves against the Brit-ish and hostile tribes. In a very real sense, therefore, the government of the United States inherited the privileges of the British crown in

1783, when the Peace of Paris transferred the territory east of the Mississippi to the former colony.

By maintaining its alliance and treaty commitments to the Indians, the United States also kept up its claim to sovereignty over this entire area. Recall that the Treaty of Paris transferred property to the United States, ninety percent of which was in Indian hands. The American colonies had yet to cross the Appalachians. Just as treaties were a statement of federal authority over the states, they were a continuing way to justify American sovereignty over the Spanish or English. If the Fort Harmar treaties had been ignored, for example, or the state of Georgia allowed to make war on the Creeks, the English in the Great Lakes or the Spanish in Florida could legitimately have intervened in defense of an embattled tribal leadership. Treaties maintained the Americans' claims to sovereignty and pre-empted outside intervention (at least under international law).

In the aftermath of the Seven Years' War, the struggle between England and France which resulted in the French expulsion from North America, the British Crown issued the Proclamation of 1763. The Proclamation is generally recalled as a contributor to the American Revolution because it prohibited American settlement beyond the Appalachians. Also important, however, is the rationale the document gives for that limit. American settlers must remain east of the mountains, the crown declared, because it was its intention to reserve the western land "under our sovereignty, protection and dominion . . . for the use of the Indians." Within the British empire, the Crown would be sovereign, even to the extent that it would "reserve" unexplored and uncharted lands "for the use" of the tribes. By continuing this British practice after the Revolution, the Americans carried on this fiction of sovereignty. The Treaty of Paris did not mention Indian sovereignty; neither did the Treaty of Ghent which ended the War of 1812, or the treaties which transferred Florida from Spain to the United States. Treaties with Indian tribes were a recognition of native leadership and a statement of national obligation to indigenous people, but they did not in themselves affect diplomacy between European powers.

Treaties were thus a product of the international diplomacy of

the colonial era and the political cross-currents of the early republic. But why were there so many of them? Why did Americans maintain the practice of negotiating treaties with Indians long after the
threat of foreign intervention or military defeat had subsided? First,
of course, the "system" worked and became routine. Commissioners were dispatched, agreements reached, and documents ratified.
Some Indian leaders valued the leverage negotiations gave them
and profited from the rewards which were often included explicitly
in treaty provisions for themselves and their friends and kin.
"Treaty chiefs" were people who gained extra-tribal recognition at
the negotiations and came to rely on the federal relationship.

Second, federal monopolization of Indian affairs proved an or-
derly way to acquire native lands. Federal authority was first tested
in Congress by legislators who opposed Washington's preference for
treaties, and later in the courts by those who wished to acquire
tribal lands without congressional authorization. This issue came
before the U.S. Supreme Court in 1823 in *Johnson v. McIntosh*.[8]
Johnson was a settler who had acquired his land directly from a
group of Illinois and Piankeshaw chiefs who later sold the same
parcel to the United States in a treaty. Federal officials then issued
homestead patents to McIntosh. Johnson sued to establish his title
based on the prior sale.

In his opinion, Chief Justice Marshall ruled against Johnson, declaring that federal supremacy in Indian affairs could not be overturned. He recognized that the tribes had the right to occupy and
enjoy their lands, but their peaceful presence within the boundaries
of the United States was a tacit recognition of federal sovereignty
and control. The chiefs could only sell their land to the United
States.

Like so many of Marshall's federalist decisions, *Johnson v. Mc-
Intosh* upheld federal power without dampening the individualistic
tendencies of his day. In the first half of the nineteenth century,
treaty commissioners and the General Land Office kept up with the
demand for more land, and federal officials played the role of facilita-
tors rather than opponents of national expansion. The great excep-
tion to this smooth process came in Georgia, where an aggressive

state government and a tenacious Cherokee tribal leadership spent two decades locked in battle. The state wanted the Indians out; the Indians, bolstered by treaties and missionaries, wanted to stay. In the end, the federal government had neither the power nor the will to resist the Georgians, but federal troops removed the Cherokees from Georgia only after government officials negotiated a treaty signed by a small minority of the tribe.

A last flurry of treaty-making took place in California and on the Great Plains just before a congressional resolution in 1871 ended the practice. These treaties harked back to the eighteenth century, where federal officials were concerned more with border chaos and expensive warfare than they were with the prerogatives of tribal governments. The California treaties—most of which Congress refused to ratify because they were too generous—were frankly drawn up to create safe havens for native people who were being gunned down in the swirl of the gold rush. The last plains agreements were produced by a series of peace commissions who were trying to insure the construction of a transcontinental railroad and to prevent a protracted guerilla war. Again, treaties were a useful format for they allowed federal officials to pre-empt local politicians while giving their actions a veneer of ideological purity.

After Congress declared (on budgetary grounds) in 1871 that no more treaties would be negotiated or signed, federal officials continued to make "agreements" with tribes that the courts have subsequently declared to have the same force as actual treaties. These documents attest to the practical value of treaty-making in the federal system. The agreements generally provide for land sales and other concessions, and they validate both federal power and the role of the Indian leaders who negotiated them.

If I ended here, readers would be correct in asking whether or not those anti-treaty Wisconsin protestors have a valid point. One may understand why there were treaties in the first place, and why treaty-making continued in the nineteenth century, but why are treaties being enforced today? Why aren't anachronistic treaties simply ignored or unilaterally abrogated?

One answer to this question is that they have frequently been ignored. The recognition of treaty rights by the federal courts is a product of recent events in both Indian history and the history of American society. For much of the twentieth century, Indian people tried in vain to get the government to recognize the legitimacy of their treaty claims; they were rebuffed.

The low point came in 1903 when a young graduate of one of the country's horrible boarding schools for Indians returned home to the Kiowa reservation and learned that Congress had sold a portion of the tribe's land without its consent. An 1867 treaty between the Kiowas and the United States had stipulated that all future land sales would require tribal approval. Drawing on his newly-acquired knowledge of civics and English, Delos Lone Wolf persuaded his father to file suit in federal court to have the land sale stopped. *Lone Wolf v. Hitchcock*[9] quickly moved to the U.S. Supreme Court which decided that on the issue of whether or not Congress could override an Indian treaty, the law was clear:

> Plenary authority over tribal relations of the Indians has been exercised by Congress from the beginning, and the power has always been deemed a political one, not subject to be controlled by the judicial department of the government. . . . The power exists to abrogate the provisions of an Indian treaty.

During this era, the courts tolerated challenges to Indian hunting and fishing rights (*Ward v. Race Horse*;[10] *U.S. v. Winans*[11], upheld federal jurisdiction over law and order within Indian communities (*U.S. v. Kagama*),[12] and rejected efforts by the so-called "Civilized Tribes" to prevent the abolition of their governments prior to the creation (in violation of a treaty) of the state of Oklahoma.

Thus, since precedence favors the abrogation of treaties even in federal courts, why have more recent rulings upheld treaty rights? Although space does not allow a detailed answer, two tentative explanations can be made. First, Indian people used the "system" to press their claims. Beginning in the 1920s there appeared a new generation of Indian leaders who understood that the American legal system could be an instrument for the protection of minority populations. Their first inclination was to file suit against the United States in the Court of Claims for various government injuries. Many of these involved either fraudulent treaties or treaties with unconscionable provisions. The most famous of the claims cases was the one filed by the various Sioux bands in the 1920s and decided in their favor by the U.S. Supreme Court in 1980. These claims cases provided tribal leaders with visibility and experience.

In the 1930s congress authorized the Indian Reorganization Act, a law which granted reservation communities the right to organize their own governments. By the 1950s many of these governments were vehicles for community social and political action as well as community governance. Tribal governments lobbied for the right to control their own schools, to run their own police departments, and to engage in ambitious economic development schemes. The story of modern tribal governments and their gradual accretion of power deserves it own book, so I will only observe that it was in 1959 that the two trends converged. The United States Supreme Court responded to a white man who sued a Navajo for debt in state court by declaring that tribal courts had original jurisdiction over such matters. It was the first recognition of the idea of tribal sovereignty in the modern era and the first of more than eighty Supreme Court decisions on Indian affairs during the next thirty-five years. The thrust of these decisions can be inferred from the following portion of one of them, *U.S. v. Wheeler*, decided on March 22, 1978:

> Before the coming of the Europeans, the tribes were self-governing sovereign political communities. . . . Like all sovereign bodies, they then had inherent power to prescribe laws for their members and to punish infractions of those laws.

> Indian tribes, are, of course, no longer possessed of the full attributes of sovereignty. . . . Their incorporation within the territory of the United States, and their acceptance of its protection, necessarily divested them of some aspects of the sovereignty which they had previously exercised. By specific treaty provision they

yielded up other sovereign powers: by statutes, in the exercise of its plenary control, Congress has removed still others.

But our cases recognize that the Indian tribes have not given up their full sovereignty. . . . The sovereignty that the tribes retain is of a unique and limited character. It exists only at the sufferance of Congress and is subject of complete defeasance. But until Congress acts, the tribes retain their existing sovereign powers.[13]

In the context of this decision, treaties become crucial indicators of what powers tribes have retained and which they have given up. Fishing and hunting rights, water rights, timber and mineral rights, rights to dance, to worship, put tribal emblems on license plates, to conduct commercial gambling operations, sell cigarettes or fishing licenses—all of these items are either "in" or "out" of that crucial bag of rights the tribes have retained. The Wheeler decision was both the culmination of decades of legal struggle, and the opening tribes needed for even more ambitious demands.

The court's phrase, "until Congress acts," points to the other change that has fostered a renaissance in Indian sovereignty. As the national government has grown in size and influence and the ethnic and racial composition of Congress has changed during the past half-century, the possibility that congressional leaders will seek to suppress tribal culture has diminished. It is still accurate to describe Congress as largely white and male and perhaps WASP to boot, but in the aftermath of the New Deal and its coalition of ethnic politicians, the civil rights movement, and the women's movement, Indian tribal governments and tribal claims can be viewed as legitimate interests in the policy-making process. A century ago, the Chairman of the Senate Committee on Indian Affairs was Henry L. Dawes of Pittsfield, Massachusetts, a pious Free-Soiler who helped found the Republican party in that state and who served as pall-bearer at Abraham Lincoln's funeral. Today it is Daniel Inouye of Honolulu, a second-generation Japanese-American who studied Thomas Jefferson in an American colony, who led the overthrow of white Republican rule in Hawaii's territorial legislature in 1954, and who has been a loyal liberal Democrat ever since. While certainly not a typical senator, Inouye reflects the social and political forces that have created modern American pluralism.

Finally, how can we reconcile treaties and the constitution's promise of equal rights for all? In trying to make sense of treaties today two elements seem crucial. First, treaties are a part of our legal culture. They have a long history, and they have been repeatedly recognized. They are on the books. They therefore carry the weight of precedent and the past. In addition to this prestige that comes with age is a moral weight. Treaties, as one legal scholar has said, are promises. While technically and legally treaties can be broken—there do come times when countries, even great countries, must break their word—our presumption is that the nation's word should be kept. Both because they are old and because they contain solemn vows, treaties cannot be dismissed lightly. Their moral claim is therefore comparable to other moral claims on the constitution—the claim that it protects our right of free speech or our right to equal protection under the law.

The second point to make about treaties and the constitution is that for Indian people treaties have become symbols of community allegiance. People affiliate with tribes of choice. Indian people who fish or hunt or sell bingo cards or tax energy companies in accord with their treaty rights do so because they choose to participate in Indian communities. Treaties reflect a part of their identity and are a tangible sign of their most personal commitments. The recognition of treaties in the constitution is therefore a recognition of the right of Indian people to affiliate as they have for centuries. Such recognition also implicitly rejects the nineteenth-century notion that Indians can do whatever they like as long as they emulate the Euro-American majority.

Because Native Americans are the only people specifically mentioned in the constitution, because their claims have a moral content, and because treaties reflect their chosen form of affiliation which the United States has frequently tried to suppress, there is no inconsistency between a recognition of Indian treaty rights and a defense of the constitution. Treaties embody choices made by the parties who sign them. They began as instruments used by weak and outnumbered Europeans to facilitate their entry into North America. They were a badge of sovereignty for Europeans. They are now an instrument wielded by weak and outnumbered Native Americans to manage their passage through the legal culture of the United States. They have become badges of Native American sovereignty. Their persistence offers hope for those who believe in rational and honorable solutions to human conflicts.

FREDERICK E. HOXIE holds the doctorate from Brandeis University and is an adjunct faculty member at both Northwestern University and the University of Illinois at Chicago. He wrote *A Final Promise: The Campaign to Assimilate the Indians, 1880–1920* and edited *Indians in American History*. Dr. Hoxie is the Director of the Newberry Library's D'Arcy McNickle Center for the History of the American Indian. Portions of the essay "Why Treaties?" are taken from his chapter in the *Final Report and Legislative Recommendations* of the Special Committee on Investigations of the Select Committee on Indian Affairs, U.S. Senate, 101 Congress, 1st Session. A preliminary version of the lecture was delivered as part of the McCloy Lectures at Amherst College, October 1990.

Notes

1. Scott Kerr, "The New Indian Wars," *The Progressive*, 54 (April, 1990): 20.

2. *American State Papers: Documents, Legislative and Executive of the Congress of the United States,* 38 volumes (Washington DC: Gales and Seaton, 1832–1861), Class 2 (Indian Affairs), volume 1, p. 13.

3. *Annals of the Congress of the United States* (Washington, D. C.), volume 1, pp. 66–72.

4. *Annals,* 81.

5. *American State Papers, Indian Affairs,* volume 1, pp. 13–14.

6. The Papal Bull *Inter Caetera,* May 4, 1493, reprinted in *Documents of American History,* 9th ed., edited by Henry Steele Commager (Englewood Cliffs, NJ, 1973), volume 1, p. 3.

7. Leslie C. Green and Olive P. Dickason, *The Law of Nations and the New World* (Edmonton, Alberta, 1989), 63.

8. Wheat. 543 (1823).

9. 187 U.S. 553 (1903).

10. 163 U.S. 504 (1896).

11. 198 U.S. 371 (1905).

12. 118 U.S. 375 (1886).

13. Francis Paul Prucha, *The Great Father: The United States Government and the American Indians II* (Lincoln, Nebraska, 1984), 1187–88.

Suggestions for Further Reading

Barsh, Russell L., and James Y. Henderson. *The Road: Indian Tribes and Political Freedom.* Berkeley: University of California Press, 1980.

Cohen, Felix. *Felix Cohen's "Handbook of Federal Indian Law."* Charlottesville, VA: Michie and Bobbs Merrill, 1982.

Cornell, Stephen. *The Return of the Native: American Indian Political Resurgence.* New York: Oxford University Press, 1988.

Deloria, Vine, Jr. *Custer Died for Your Sins: An Indian Manifesto.* Norman: University of Oklahoma Press, 1988. Reprint of 1969 edition (New York, Macmillan).

Deloria, Vine, Jr., ed. *American Indian Policy in the Twentieth Century.* Norman: University of Oklahoma Press, 1985.

Deloria, Vine, Jr., and Clifford M. Lytle. *The Nations Within: The Past and Future of American Indian Sovereignty.* New York: Pantheon Books, 1984.

DeMallie, Raymond J. "Touching the Pen: Plains Indian Treaty Councils in Ethnohistorical Perspective," in *Ethnicity on the Great Plains*, edited by Frederick C. Luebke, pp. 38–53. Lincoln: University of Nebraska Press, 1980.

Dippie, Brian W. *The Vanishing American: White Attitudes and U.S. Indian Policy.* Middletown, CT: Wesleyan University Press, 1982.

Edmunds, R. David. *The Shawnee Prophet.* Lincoln: University of Nebraska Press, 1983.

Hoxie, Frederick E. *A Final Promise: The Campaign to Assimilate the Indians, 1880–1920.* Lincoln: University of Nebraska Press, 1984; Cambridge: Cambridge University Press, 1989.

Jennings, Francis. *The Invasion of America: Indians, Colonialism, and the Cant of Conquest.* Chapel Hill: University of North Carolina Press for the Institute of Early American History and Culture, 1975.

Josephy, Alvin M, Jr., ed. *America in 1492: The World of the Indian Peoples before the Arrival of Columbus.* 2nd ed. New York: Vintage, 1993.

Kelly, Lawrence C. *The Assault on Assimilation: John Collier and the Origins of Indian Policy Reform.* Albuquerque: University of New Mexico Press, 1983.

Prucha, Francis Paul. *The Great Father: The United States Government and the American Indians.* 2 vols. Lincoln: University of Nebraska Press, 1986.

Taylor, Graham D. *The New Deal and American Indian Tribalism: The Administration of the Indian Reorganization Act, 1934–1945.* Lincoln: University of Nebraska Press, 1980.

White, Richard, *The Middle Ground: Indians, Empires and Republics in the Great Lakes Region, 1650–1815.* New York: Cambridge University Press, 1991.

Wilkinson, Charles F. *American Indians, Time and Law: Native Societies in a Modern Constitutional Democracy.* New Haven: Yale University Press, 1987.

Lithograph of *View of the Great Treaty Held at Prairie du Chien, September 1825,* painted on the spot by James Otto Lewis. Treaty Commissioners William Clark of Missouri and Lewis Cass of Michigan met with "upwards of 5,000 warriors." At this large intertribal gathering two western political leaders attempted to broker a peace between such rivals as the Ojibwas and the Dakotas, and to persuade Indians of the region to sign a multilateral document specifying boundaries between tribes; both necessary preparations for subsequent land cession treaties. Photo courtesy the State Historical Society of Wisconsin. WHi(X3)2812.

Priests and nuns at the "Jubilate Deo, 1835–1935," Red Cliff Ojibwa community, Apostle Islands, Wisconsin, 1935. Photo courtesy State Historical Society of Wisconsin. WHi(X3)36912.

A Native American acting group toured Wisconsin in 1994. The Wisconsin Indian Story Theatre enacted stories from the oral legends of each tribe in Wisconsin. The amateur actors are shown performing *The Ice Man and the Messenger.* Photo by Bjorn Olson, University of Wisconsin–Madison News and Public Affairs.

Tree-tapping maple syrup ceremony, Oneida, Wisconsin. Photo courtesy Oneida Communications, Oneida, Wisconsin.

Oneida language contest at the Norbert Hill Center auditorium, February 25, 1994. Photo courtesy Oneida Communications, Oneida, Wisconsin.

George Whitewing is seated at the drum in Red Cloud Park, Jackson County, Wisconsin. Photo by John Froelich, courtesy the State Historical Society of Wisconsin. WHi(X32)20504.

Survival This Way:

Indian Policy and Living Tradition

Thomas Vennum, Jr.

Center for Folklife Programs
and Cultural Studies
Smithsonian Institution

An Ojibwa chief recalled the negotiations leading to the St. Peter's treaty of 1837 in the following words: "That you may not destroy the wild rice in working the timber, also the rapids and falls in the stream I will lend to you to saw your timber. Also a small tract of land to make a garden to live on while you are working the timber. I do not make you a present of this. I merely lend it to you. This is my answer. My Great Father is great, and out of respect for him I will not refuse him, but as an exchange of civility I must see and feel the benefits of this loan and the promises fulfilled."

Traditional lifestyles throughout the world depend upon a myriad of factors for their survival. While we may take their continuation for granted, our oblivious attitude to environmental dangers is paralleled by our ignorance of threats to the equally fragile cultural ecosystem. The healthy survival of certain crafts, for instance, depends upon a correct alignment of social and economic agendas with the natural environment. For example, the colliding interests of Indians and non-Indians threaten Great Basin basketry traditions of Nevada tribes. Housing developers have already plowed under much of the Truckee Meadows willow habitat. Where once the Paiute, Shoshone, and Washoe customarily moved out early each spring to collect willow stems alongside streams where the bush grew naturally, today most remaining willow is on restricted private property, fenced in for cattle grazing or farming. In the arid climate of Nevada the willow, a thirsty bush, competes with cattle for limited water, so ranchers have attempted full-scale eradication of the plant, weeding it out or spraying it with herbicides. Traditional basketry technology requires splitting stems lengthwise into splints, and the centuries-old means of doing so involves holding one end of the stem between the teeth. Thus basketmakers, even if they can find willows, risk exposing themselves to toxic chemicals in working with the material. Decreasing access to willow and the well-grounded fear of its contamination discourage Nevada Indians from searching it out. Many have given up basketmaking as a result.

Each summer my office at the Smithsonian mounts the Festival of American Folklife on the National Mall. Two years ago, as curator, I developed a program entitled "American Indian Problems of Access and Cultural Continuity." It addressed head-on the entire issue of access in a broadly conceived interpretation of the term. Simply put, what are the problems Indian people face in maintaining their traditional cultures and thus a significant part of their cultural identity as tribes and individuals? Almost always the answer will identify impediments imposed by the dominant Euro-American society, which is motivated by economic, political, or social considerations. Access to natural materials such as willows is an obvious problem; others are more subtle.

General despoilment of the environment and exploitation of natural resources on the American continent have resulted in the disappearance of many animal and plant species long held sacred by Native Americans—species ritually required in religious ceremonies and healing, often providing the very basis of a tribe's material culture. Along the Northwest coast, for example, the clear-cutting of vast stands of old-growth redwood and cedar by the lumber industry has impinged on the native cultures of the area, who formerly used the timber for canoes, longhouses, and totemic figures, and the bark for medicine, clothing, dyes, baskets, and musical instruments.

Although industry has reseeded many clear-cut areas, they have planted Douglas fir which grows much faster and can be harvested earlier for profit. Meanwhile, the increasing value of cedar and redwood as ornamental wood for Japanese furniture and rot-resistant American patio and sundeck construction hastens their decline. The people who for centuries have lived among the northwest coastal forests no longer have access to such materials. For them, these life-giving trees were sacred, figured prominently in their legends and belief systems, and were treated accordingly with respect rather than exploited for commercial advantage.

Our program also addressed access to traditional food sources. When the government forcibly settled American Indians on reservations, it often chose land far removed from their traditional homelands. Foods customarily associated with their subsistence economies—especially wild game—were no longer available. Restricted by reservation boundaries, Indians found the more practical—or the only—alternative was to turn to the canned goods of the dominant society. Elders expressed a general distaste for these items, often citing their consumption as a cause of poor health. Complained Josephine Clark of Leech Lake Reservation in Minnesota. "Well, long time ago people didn't get sick like they do now, you know. Sometimes I blame the food we eat now. Maybe it's the food that does it. . . . See, the Indians all had their land, they had wild potatoes, they had wild rice, they had maple sugar, they had deer meat, they had ducks, all these wild stuff you know, they eat. They never bought anything from canned stuff. And they fixed their food their own way."[1]

Indian access to recognition from American society was perhaps the most subtle of themes with which our program dealt. Ironically, our educational system rarely reminds Americans of the debt owed to the original inhabitants of the continent. Indian people began sharing their foodstuffs before the first Thanksgiving at Plymouth; later they showed how to cultivate corn—a crop now at the foundation of American agriculture and the world economy. They taught centuries-old technologies and never-bettered strategies for survival in the wilderness, from making canoes, snowshoes, and toboggans to tapping maple trees for sugar and harvesting pumpkins, squash, and wild rice. The symbiotic relationship that developed between Indians, the military, furtraders, and missionaries was essential to the westward expansion and development of the North American continent.

To address the question of access to recognition, we brought spokespersons from the Iroquois Nation. Through competition in games on the National Mall and in workshops on our narrative stage, they reminded visitors that the game of lacrosse, increasingly popular on high school and college campuses, was originally an Indian sport. Intricately bound up with legend and ceremony, lacrosse was played by Indians throughout the eastern half of North America at the time of European contact—a fact little known or credited to the Indian, even by many who now play the game. When the Olympic Committee stripped the great Indian athlete Jim Thorpe of his Olympic medals, its action was as racially motivated as the National Lacrosse Association's 1880 decision to declare Indians "professionals" and effectively exclude them from international competition for a century.

———

The problems of access began with the arrival of Europeans in what Indian people (and some historians) have come to refer to as "The Invasion of North America." In the process of colonization and increasing territorial expansion, cultures inevitably collided, with subsequent displacement of native peoples. Fur trade economic forces and the zeal of missionaries drove Ojibwas living at the east end of Lake Superior at the time of contact to become middlemen and guides for traders and missionaries, and their language became the *lingua franca* of barter throughout the western Great Lakes.

Acquiring firearms from traders, they systematically drove out less powerful peoples such as the Dakota, and Michigan Algonquins to their west.

Americans viewed Indians as inferior "savages" whose way of life and landbase interfered with frontier expansion, which was justified by the theory of "Manifest Destiny." In the nineteenth century, federal policy-makers adopted a number of expedient but drastic measures to solve "the Indian problem." These ranged from concentrating Indian populations onto reservations and thereby acquiring their former lands and restricting their movements to removing them to distant territories, as when federal troops forced southeastern tribes to march on foot in "The Trail of Tears" to present-day Oklahoma in the late 1830s. In some cases, local sentiment favored outright genocide as the only solution, such as the attempted extermination of the Apaches in the Southwest. In our 1989 Festival program, the Yaqui participants descended from political refugees who fled north from Sonora, Mexico, in the early twentieth century, when soldiers deliberately attempted to kill off the tribe.

The very circumstances under which reservations were created affect current problems of access. Usually government officials selected land deemed "unsuitable" for non-Indian needs, which often meant barren or rocky topography—useless for farming or lumbering. In one of the greatest recent ironies, five of the twelve sites initially selected by the U.S. Department of Energy for dumpsites to contain radioactive waste were on Indian land, one of them belonging by treaty to the Menominee. When federal agents plotted the Menominee Reservation it did not include Lake Shawano, traditionally their source of wild rice. The new reservation land was so rocky that it precluded farming as a substitute for the loss of wild rice, their traditional subsistence crop. But a century later, government energy bureaucrats eyed the Wolf River batholith on the reservation covetously as the perfect crystalline rock to contain nuclear waste.

Most reservations resulted from treaties entered into between Indians and the federal government. In surrendering vast tracts of their lands, Indians hoped that whites merely wished to extract timber and minerals from the areas and then perhaps move on. Even when land opened for settlement by non-Indian immigrants, Indians were adamant and specific about their continued right to practice aboriginal pursuits on ceded territories, and that they remain perpetually free to hunt, fish, forage, and gather materials. As Chief Martin of the Ottawa Lake Ojibwa protested to the governor of Wisconsin Territory in 1843: "We have no objections to the white man's working the mines and the timber and making farms. But we reserve the birch bark and cedar, for canoes, the wild rice and maple sugar trees, and the privilege of hunting without being disturbed by the whites."

For many reasons, Indian people seldom attempted until recently to exercise fully these off-reservation rights. In court cases, treaty language—never very clear even in the nineteenth-century negotiations—has been interpreted and reinterpreted, not always in the Indians' favor. Still, following certain landmark federal court decisions, such as the Voigt decision affecting northern Wisconsin, Indian people now find free access to practices and resources that have gone untapped for more than a century. In newly attempting to exercise their old reserved rights—be they salmon fishing in Washington, or out-of-season deer hunting and off-reservation fish spearing in Wisconsin—or even to regain territories illegally taken from them, such as Oneida lands in New York, native peoples have engendered a new wave of resentment from their non-Indian neighbors, leading to protests, demonstrations, and even ugly physical confrontations. Upstate New Yorkers, outraged over Cayuga land claims, fail to understand why they should be affected by historical legalities they known nothing about; northern Wisconsin sportfishers are angered when Ojibwas spear walleyes and muskies—a right reserved in their 1854 treaty and upheld in court. Insisting that they should not be affected by events more than a century ago, opponents to spear fishing have formed anti-treaty rights groups. "This is 1991," they argue, "not 1854." Gaining access to the law and justice in redressing wrongs has been a long and arduous struggle for Indian people.

Reservations were but one solution to the "The Indian Problem." In the latter half of the nineteenth century, programs to assimilate

Indians into the great American "melting pot" intensified. Ultimately policy-makers aimed to award them citizenship and suffrage rights that accompanied that privilege. To prepare their entry into society, policy-makers made every effort to eradicate their traditional cultures. Missionaries moved onto reservations to stamp out "heathen" religious practices; Indian children were trooped off to federal boarding schools, where they were deliberately intermixed with children from other tribes, forbidden from wearing traditional dress and given uniforms, punished for speaking their native tongues, and otherwise forced to conform to a non-Indian model.

Meanwhile, the reservations themselves—the last remaining landbase for most tribes—came under siege with the Dawes General Allotment Act of 1887, which effectively broke up communally-held reservation property by alloting the land to individuals. Ostensibly this was to instill a "free-enterprise" spirit in Indians, induce them to take up farming in place of traditional hunting and foraging, and encourage personal initiative over tribal decisions. In actuality, though, the act resulted in further division and demoralization among Indians. Many predictably sold off their allotments for short-term gains, and land-grabbing by unscrupulous entrepreneurs siphoned off much of the rest. Today, many reservations resemble "checkerboards" of white/Indian tracts. In some instances, tribes now own less than ten percent of their original reservations.

In addressing the history of the access problem, we must contrast the Euro-American concept of land use with Indian attitudes towards land and property. Although the majority of tribes in the East as well as riverine peoples on the Plains were settled agriculturalists, Europeans conveniently regarded Indians as nomadic peoples, roaming over large areas of land at will. There were no Indian mechanisms for surveying land to establish boundaries, no maps to delineate ownership, no fences or walls to contain properties; indeed, the very concept of private land was foreign to Indians. Indians nevertheless had a very accurate sense of geography based on topographical and other physical features. They relied on natural boundaries, such as rivers, mountains, lakes, and other landmarks, or they knew special areas to contain certain species. Although individuals did not own land itself they could claim its resources. Indian people had various means of indicating usufructuary rights to certain areas: they marked the trees in a maple sugar grove with a distinguishing slash of an axe, or they sheaved and bound wild rice on a lake using some distinctive twist or colored yarn to indicate the customary harvesting areas of a particular family. Indians understood winter trapping areas similarly, and Indian customary law dealt severely with transgressions by outsiders.

At the root of Europeans' consternation was the failure to appreciate Indian ideas that land was communally and not personally owned. This explains why sovereign Indian nations, not individuals, press Indian land claims in courts today. In fact, an elaborate political interrelationship based on kinship operated to *ensure* property in communality, such as the marriage alliances binding together the Six Nations of the Iroquois Confederacy. Oblivious to these principles of ownership and sharing, Europeans were used instead to systems of private sedentary agriculture. What appeared on the surface to be perpetual nomadism needed to be checked or contained, Europeans asserted, if the continent were to be "properly" developed.

To survive, many Indian people *had* to move in pursuit of food sources because they practiced a subsistence economy. Developed over centuries, their strategy for survival naturally led them to change locations seasonally, as each item—animal or vegetal— "ripened." In the case of the Ojibwa, for whom wild rice was foremost a vital staple but later paramount in value as a trade item, a seasonal rhythm had evolved, closely synchronized with the natural environment. In the summer months, Ojibwas gathered in villages by lakes or rivers, fishing, gardening, and berry gathering. In late summer they moved to the wild rice lakes to harvest, process, and store rice for their winter needs. Then, in late fall, they traveled to areas most heavily populated with deer for their hunting. During the winter months they fanned out in single family units to hunting and trapping territories—each area large enough to ensure a sufficient game supply for the winter. Come spring they moved into the sugar bush to tap maple trees. With the arrival of summer they re-turned to the lakeside villages, and the cycle began anew.

Forced settlement on reservations drastically reduced the Ojib-wa's ability to pursue their traditional subsistence economy and threatened their food supply. When U.S. officials drew reservation boundaries, they often excluded the band's traditional rice lakes or sugar groves. Trapping and hunting diminished, and they became increasingly reliant on the foodstuffs of the dominant society. As a hedge against wild rice failures on the reservation, and taking advan-tage of the fact that treaties protected foraging rights even on territo-ries ceded to the government, Ojibwas began deliberately to sow wild rice seed in rivers and lakes previously lacking stands.

As settlers poured into the newly ceded territories, converting forests to farmland, they destroyed much of the former habitat of natural species. The resulting loss of game only exacerbated the situation for Indian people, as they continued to be deprived of the natural resources that had been the foundation of their traditional culture. Skills and craft traditions became obsolete, as the natural materials disappeared; the harvesting of birch trees for pulpwood, for example, hastened the decline of canoe-making. Today in the western Great Lakes region one can rarely find birch trees large enough to supply the bark needed for a canoe. As loggers cut spruce forests and removed stumps to render the land tillable, Ojibwa lost access to spruce roots used traditionally to sew together bark sheets for wigwams, canoes, and pails. Spruce stumps—ideal for parching wild rice because of their slow, steady burn—were no longer available.

One justification given in dispossessing Indians of their land was that they were not using it to its fullest productivity. This old European land-use theory continues to plague the world—its appli-cation in Brazil is the driving force of genocide throughout the Amazon rainforests today. What the theory ignores is that Indians maintained a proper balance with their natural environment, prac-ticed ecologically sound economies, and produced sustained yields for most of their needs. This approach is at odds with the Western obsession to increase crop production and to harvest every last kernel. When these methods were applied to former Indian staples, the result often met with disaster. For example, Ojibwas had mainly harvested only enough wild rice for their own needs; they allowed remaining kernels to shell out naturally into the lake, fall to the bottom, and reseed the bed for the following year's crop. In fact, the traditional Indian means of harvesting rice by knocking ripened kernels with flails into a canoe guaranteed that a good portion of the seed rice fell into the water. The Indians had always recognized this as good resource management, but, incredibly, in Minnesota the Department of Natural Resources described the Indian harvesting methods as "wasteful" in that so much of the crop was lost to the lake.

One of the principal access problems facing Ojibwa people today concerns wild rice. It is mainly an economic issue of fair access to marketing. While there are other problems surrounding the healthy maintenance of this crop—endangerment from the ever-spreading purple loosestrife plant, artificial water levels controlled by governments and private power companies, pollution threats by mining, none of these has yet had as devastating an impact on the Ojibwa as the recent flooding of the market with cheap, artificially-produced paddy rice. One of my predictions in my 1988 book on wild rice has unfortunately come to pass, that is, that many Ojibwa have given up ricing altogether, thereby severing an important cultural link to their past. Faced with a glut in the paddy rice market caused mostly by vast overproduction in California, growers have resorted to the insidious practice of dumping paddy rice at fire-sale prices in areas near Indian reservations. They retail it in taverns, gas stations, and out of roadside vans. It is flown into Minnesota and Wisconsin from California, packaged with Indian canoe or lakeside-scene emblems to disguise its artificial origins, then dumped at $1.60 a pound. The strategy of doing this near reservations is clear. The average tourist driving by is oblivious to any distinctions between natural, hand-processed rice and paddy rice. He need only to compare the $6.00 a pound sign he has seen on the reservation to think he is getting the same product at a bargain. The problem for Indians is that this strategy is working, despite the efforts to enforce labelling laws. To understand the problem, it is necessary to review the economic history of the Indians' relationship to this crop, which I do at some length in my book, *Wild Rice and the Ojibway People.*

At the root of many Indian problems of access to resources is the prevailing non-Indian attitude towards the natural world—that it exists to be exploited by humans for short-term personal wealth and pleasure. However, we should not romanticize "the noble Indian as ecologist." Indians practiced sound conservation for pragmatic reasons. Although their respect for nature was reflected in various rituals, such as "first fruits" thanksgivings, or in actions such as putting a pinch of tobacco as an offering in the ground when removing some root or plant or apologizing to a bear before killing it, their motives were as much practical as spiritual.

Recent ethnohistorical studies of Indian resource management suggest that Indians strategically planned to use "gifts" of nature for the well-being of the community; they gave special attention to prevent the resource from being strained or depleted, thereby ensuring the same bounty for future generations. Today, overproduction leading to depletion of resources is but one of the threats to the natural environment, depriving Indian people of traditional foods and materials. Waste and pollution are equally culpable. The wanton slaughter of bison—often merely for target practice from moving trains—had a devastating effect on many Plains tribes, whose culture so totally depended upon this animal. Once numbering nearly fifty million, the bison were brought to the verge of extinction—at one time only several hundred survived. Often the only body parts desired by non-Indians were bison tongues, a table delicacy, and furs for lap robes; the carcasses were simply left to rot. Indians viewed such waste as sacrilege. For them nearly every part of the animal had some use. Even dried dung was an essential fuel on the treeless Plains. After a kill, meat that Indians did not consume fresh on the spot was preserved for future use; sun-dried for jerky, or dried, pounded and mixed with fat for pemmican. Indians sewed together hides for tipis or tanned them for moccasins and other apparel, converted sinews into "Indian thread," and twisted together tendons for cordage; they even used the stomach pouch and the heart skin as containers. Bones they made into tools, and the buffalo skull they retained for use in sacred ceremonies of the Sun Dance. When the government forced Plains tribes onto reservations, as part of their treaty rights it promised annuities that included food supplies. Due to the near extinction of the bison, government agents substituted beef cattle in their annual rations to the Sioux.

Pollution of all sorts has deprived Indians of access to traditional resources and occupations. Mineral tailings, oil spills, acid rain, herbicides, and pesticides have all adversely affected the food chain and rendered inedible foods formerly relied upon. Mercury dumping by a paper mill in Dryden, Ontario, so severely contaminated the river system that commercial fishing had to be banned by the government; summer resorts closed, so Indian fishing guides became unemployed. The Exxon mineral finds in northeastern Wisconsin could well pollute Mole Lake downstream, the principal wild rice resource for Sokaogan Ojibwa. Similarly, the Kennecott copper interests threaten the Flambeau River. The establishment of canneries in the 1890s in Alaskan areas of sea otter concentration fouled the environment and caused the animals to abandon their hauling grounds, areas where marine animals habitually congregate when they leave the water.

Another form of pollution—the introduction of exotic species and diseases—has also taken its toll. Coastal Indians in eastern Canada may have been exposed to deadly viruses and bacteria by European fishermen long before the "discovery" of America. Early records of the Jesuits confirm the high mortality rate of native populations once infected by smallpox and influenza against which they had no immunity. Exotic plants and animals introduced to the New World habitat by non-Indians often threatened indigenous species upon which Indians relied. Russians introduced foxes throughout the western Aleutian Islands to harvest for their pelts. Unchecked and rapidly multiplying, the foxes became a menace to the native bird populations that the Aleuts required for food and clothing. "German" carp, a species that feeds on roots, threaten wild rice plants; in some beds rice competes with purple loosestrife, an exotic plant. As the American frontier moved west, cattle and sheep raisers usurped the grazing areas of natural species, such as bison and elk; and where natural species such as eagles, wolves, or coyotes threatened newly imported ones, farmers and ranchers destroyed the native species by poisoned baits and other means.

In a particularly outrageous action touching on the access issue, cattlemen in Wyoming in 1971 killed more than five hundred eagles from helicopters, claiming the birds to be predators on lambs, when, in fact, eagles only rarely prey on livestock. The irony of that event is a particularly bitter one to Indian people, whose access to eagle feathers is severely hindered by laws protecting endangered species. While law enforcement agents were slow to prosecute ranchers for wanton eagle slaughter, federal agents in Oklahoma agressively applied the laws by arresting twenty-two Indians and six non-Indians, bringing them to trial and convicting them for possession of eagle feathers. The eagle is a sacred bird to most Indians, its feathers symbolizing life itself. For centuries Indians have incorporated eagle feathers into sacred ritual paraphernalia and badges of honor. Now the onus of proof is on Indians to show that feathers in their possession are exclusively for religious purposes.

At the same time denying Indian people access to elements of their traditional cultures, the dominant society redefined "the Indian" according to its own dictates. We have selected items from Indian culture to form stereotypes that have then been exploited for commercial purposes in a number of ways. Concurrently, America was expropriating what it could of Indian cultural elements. I have mentioned the game of lacrosse. Sculpted Indian figures emerged to hold cigars before tobacco shops; sports teams continue to incorporate the stoic "fighting" image by being named "Braves" or "Warriors"; many Indian people cringe today watching the antics of the feathered, war-bonneted mascot at Washington Redskins football games or the Atlanta baseball fans' "tomahawk chop." Indian musical themes, some of them sacred in origin, were grist for American composers, who expropriated them from their usual contexts and gave them Western harmonic settings in their "Indian Suites." One Indian melody, in fact a sacred song of the Native American Church, was borrowed as a jingle-tune to advertise carpeting. Topline fashion designers turn to turquoise, silver, buckskin, and classic Indian patterns to combine them into expensive cocktail attire. For an automobile we accept the name choice and symbol design of "Thunderbird"—a powerful spirit in Indian sacred beliefs—but we would recoil should Detroit venture to call its latest model a "Jesusmobile."

By raising the issue of Indian access, we can stimulate further dialogue between Indian people and the general public. More attention needs to be paid those aspects of their culture that they feel cut off from, through education and increased media attention. Indians in many places have initiated their own solutions to these problems.

Indian resource management is increasingly a viable alternative to federal and state control over traditional resources. Successful wildlife management efforts on many reservations have demonstrated Indians' ability to produce sustained annual yields without succumbing to the temptations of short-term gains. After nearly a century of absence, bison and elk herds have been reintroduced on Plains Indian reservations. The National Park Service has cooperated with tribes in moving animals from overstocked herds, such as in Yellowstone Park, to establish new herds on reservations under the supervision of tribal wildlife managers. Problems do attend such efforts; ranges must be carved from existing cattle grazing areas and heavily fenced in, not only to contain the buffalo herd but to protect it against poaching. Modern veterinary attention must check diseases, and the herd must be culled periodically to keep it at manageable size. To assist funding for herd management, South Dakota Sioux have implemented occasional trophy hunts, both for outside game hunters as well as local residents selected through lotteries. Buffalo meat is gaining increased popularity throughout the country as a rich protein source low in fat; many who have tried it prefer it to beef, and a consumer market is slowly developing for this resource. Meanwhile, as in the old days, some bison are slaughtered by tribal people for feasts, and fresh bison skulls are now available for the sacred Sun Dance, which is enjoying a resurgence on the Plains. The general attitude expressed by Dakotan people shows an appreciation for this renewed contact with their past culture; most say it makes them feel good "just having the buffalo around." Success with bison reintroduction is leading to similar efforts with elk and big-horn sheep.

Elsewhere, Indian groups have banded together to attack common access problems. Based on the Bad River Reservation, in Wisconsin, the Great Lakes Indian Fish and Wildlife Commission, whose membership now includes eight reservations from three states, has been active on the conservation front through annual meetings and its bi-monthly publication, *Masinaigan*, the Ojibwa word for newspaper. They support dialogue with state departments of natural resources and enlist the services of university researchers in many activities: developing fish hatcheries to restock lakes, studying the threats to wild rice beds from exotic plant species and fish, reintroducing a number of bird species, exploring pollution control and easement possibilities along vital streams, and conducting a general education campaign through public forums. Combating racism has become an essential goal in the wake of tensions and confrontations ensuing from treaty rights decisions.

Meanwhile, access issues continue to plague Indian cultures in many areas. Craftspeople who receive but a fraction of the retail price of their products, given the enormous markup of middlemen, must develop improved marketing possibilities. Some solutions must be found for marketing Indian-processed natural foods like wild rice. And Indian sacred places, from Blue Lake in New Mexico to the High Country of northern California, must be preserved and protected from the threats of development for ski resorts or from being cut off from Indian people by construction of logging highways. Legislation needs to be enacted to stop clear-cutting of National Forests and oil-drilling in Alaskan caribou habitat. Federal agencies must more aggressively prosecute environmental violations adversely affecting Indian traditions, such as illegal, covert logging on Indian land and destruction of endangered species by farmers and ranchers. In this way we can redress the many wrongs that have prevented Indian people from practicing these traditions so vital to a healthy culture, for only when people regain control of their cultural tools can they begin to deal effectively with the many social and economic problems facing them.

Portions of this essay have been excerpted from *Wild Rice and the Ojibway People* (Minnesota Historical Society Press, 1988) and "American Indian Problems of Access and Cultural Continuity," *1989 Festival of American Folklife* (program book, Smithsonian Institution), both by Thomas Vennum, Jr.

An expert on Ojibwa ethnomusicology, **THOMAS VENNUM, JR.**, earned a doctorate at Harvard University. His study of wild rice in Ojibwa culture and his monograph in the Smithsonian Folklife series entitled *The Ojibwa Dance Drum: Its History and Construction* are models of modern scholarship on the Ojibwa people. Dr. Vennum is currently in the Center for Folklife Programs and Cultural Studies at the Smithsonian Institution.

Note

1. Ojibwa novelist Louise Erdrich exploits this common Indian attitude toward 'wild' vs. 'storebought' food when Lipsha Morrissey feeds his grandfather a love potion made of frozen grocery-store turkey hearts instead of wild geese hearts, and his grandfather chokes to death (*Love Medicine*, New York, 1984).

Suggestions for Further Reading

Vennum, Thomas, Jr. *Wild Rice and the Ojibway People.* St. Paul: Minnesota Historical Society Press, 1988.

Vennum, Thomas, Jr. *The Ojibwa Dance Drum: Its History and Construction.* Washington, DC: Smithsonian Institution Press, 1982.

Tribal Sovereignty and Natural Resources:

The Lac Courte Oreilles Experience

James W. Oberly

University of Wisconsin–Eau Claire

A t certain points in history, time and space come together to highlight change in human affairs. Such moments in time are outlined in bolder relief when a region and a people are transformed through environmental change, economic development, and social conflict. Northern Wisconsin during and after the lumbering era was such a place and time. More precisely, the dam project completed at Winter, Wisconsin, in 1923 to create the Chippewa Flowage in Sawyer County has a history that for over a century tied together three of the main themes in Wisconsin history.

First, the project produced changes in the environment, especially for the watersheds of one of the state's principal rivers between the end of the Civil War and the 1920s; indeed, the recent use of the term "conquest" to interpret the history of the trans-Mississippi West aptly applies to the environmental history of northern Wisconsin's cut-over region as well. Second, the dam project involved extensive interaction between federal and state governmental agencies and business of the Progressive Era. To a certain extent, the dam was a part of the "Wisconsin Idea," if that concept may be defined as the aggressive use of state government to further economic development. Third, the dam project took place in part on Indian land and the subsequent destruction of the old settlement of Pahquawong (also known as "The Post") thus belongs to the larger history of "dammed Indians" in the twentieth century, as well as the specific history of the Ojibwas at a time when the State of Wisconsin successfully sought to limit the treaty rights enjoyed by the Tribe in the nineteenth century.[1]

The Winter Dam and Chippewa Flowage project in northern Wisconsin is an example of land and water use that has provoked conflict several times in the twentieth century. For almost seventy years after its construction, the dam continued as an ongoing legal and political controversy. Following World War I, whites in Wisconsin, Minnesota, and in Washington, D. C., wanted the dam built, and a band of Indians whose reservation was partially flooded by the dam did not. An immediate result of the dam's construction was the inundation of the place the Ojibwa Indians called Pahquahwong (or "Pak-wa-wong") roughly translated as "the place where the river is wide," near the junction of the East and West Forks of the Chippewa River.

The dam's history goes beyond past local politics. Moreover, it is the history of conflicting attitudes about the most desirable economic system, set within a framework of racial conflict between Wisconsin whites and the Ojibwa (or "Chippewa" or "Anishinaabe") Indians. This study puts the history of the dam into the larger context of the Progressive Era, and explains the participants in their own terms.[2]

The chronology of the Winter Dam begins in the Jacksonian Era when the Lake Superior Band of Chippewa Indians signed a series of treaties with the United States, ceding much of the land of northern Michigan, Wisconsin, and Minnesota to federal control in return for annuity payments and certain reserved rights. In 1837, Henry

Dodge, the territorial governor and former militia commander in the Black Hawk War, led a U.S. delegation to meet members of the Mississippi and Lake Superior bands of Ojibwas at St. Peter (now St. Paul) in the then Wisconsin Territory. After days of delay and wrangling, Dodge concluded what contemporaries called the "Pine Treaty," so called because the Ojibwas sold a considerable portion of Wisconsin to the U.S. with the understanding from Dodge that whites wanted to log the timber on the land, not farm it. Five years later, the U.S. secured another treaty from the Tribe granting federal control to the lands on much of the south shore of Lake Superior, this time with the acknowledged reason being access to the copper and other mineral deposits. In the last of these treaties, concluded in 1854 at La Pointe, the Ojibwas ceded much of their landholdings in northern Minnesota to U.S. control. It also set up several reservations for the Ojibwas and explicitly reversed earlier U.S. policy of compelling the scattered bands to remove from Wisconsin to Indian Country on the Great Plains. The most populous of the reservations set aside from the ceded land was at Lac Courte Oreilles (or "Lake Short Ears"), on the upper Chippewa River near the hamlet of Winter, about 125 miles northeast of St. Paul, at a site that had been an active fur-trading post since the early eighteenth century.[3]

The Ojibwas of Pahquahwong and Lac Courte Oreilles had maintained an existence based on hunting, fishing, trapping, and gathering at least since the mid-eighteenth century. By the time of the mid-nineteenth-century treaties, we begin to get good written accounts of the diet and economy of the Lake Superior Ojibwas. For example, under the terms of the 1837 treaty, the U.S. paid for the services of three blacksmiths for the Tribe, with one of their principal tasks being to forge fishing-spears and traps. Daniel Bushnell, the Indian agent at La Pointe despaired about ever converting his charges into agriculturalists when he wrote in 1840 that the Ojibwas "subsist at present by hunting, fishing, and on the wild rice found in the lakes and rivers," although he added ominously that the resources "are generally failing and must ultimately become inadequate." Further east a few years later, one of the surveyors on the Owen expedition of 1847 wrote that the Indians at Lac du Flambeau "raise excellent potatoes, better, indeed, than are usually grown, with all the aids of civilization, in the valley of Ohio," but he added, "their principal dependence for food is upon the lake, which yields them a plentiful supply of fine fish."[4]

Supplemented by annual treaty-annuity payments, the hunting and fishing economy continued throughout the Civil War years. The agent at La Pointe reported in July, 1863, that the "Indians had all left on their Summer hunt," and by October he requested a winter "furlough" to Connecticut from the Indian Office in Washington, as the Ojibwas "usually go on their hunting trips about the first of Nov. and there is usually but little business requiring the presence of the Agent during the Winter." Anthropologist Frances Densmore, who did her field work among the Ojibwas of White Earth, Minnesota, and Lac Courte Oreilles, counted over one hundred different plants used for food and medicine or as what she called a "utility," such as birch bark for canoes.[5] The massive logging operations carried out by Frederick Weyerhaeuser and other lumbermen also produced far-reaching changes in the northern Wisconsin environment. The environmental transformation in turn had important consequences for Ojibwa ways of hunting, fishing, and gathering. By 1905, for example, the State Forester inspected three Chippewa reservations and found Lac du Flambeau suffered from poor soil and "fearfully wasteful" cut-over lands; likewise, at Lac Courte Oreilles, the land was "very heavily cut and burned over" and not suitable for farming. The Bad River reservation; which had lost 150 million board feet of timber to fire, had some good soils, but the State Forester wrote knowingly of the Ojibwas: "As anyone can testify who has become acquainted with them, they do not seem to have any faculty or taste for farming, but are more inclined to work in the woods than anywhere else."[6]

Preliminary Moves

The geology of the Chippewa Valley divides neatly into two halves, a Cambrian lower valley where the river is wide and placid, and a pre-Cambrian upper river above present-day Chippewa Falls, where the river drops 550 feet within one hundred miles. The geology, topography, and resources of northern Wisconsin and the upper Chippewa Valley had long interested scientific parties exploring the region. Henry Dodge, of course, was informed about the extent of pine forests growing in the northern half of the Wisconsin Territory when he negotiated with the Ojibwas in 1837. He had relied on the reports of the Indian Office's Henry Schoolcraft and other travelers. In setting up a land district for northern Wisconsin, the General Land Office sent geologist David Dale Owen in 1847 to explore the valley and the south shore of Lake Superior. Owen commented favorably on the prospects for logging the pineries, but doubted if agricultural settlers would find much of a field for operations in the region. One problem he noted was the profusion "of venomous insects, in such insufferable quantities, that at certain seasons, they destroy all comfort on a quiet day," and mosquitoes once attacked his companions in such force that their "ears swelled to two or three times their natural size, and the line of our hats marked, all round, by the trickling blood." Northern portions of the state, he concluded, were "scarcely habitable, except by a race, like the Chippewa Indians, content to subsist on fish, wild rice, and the sugar of the maple." Subsequent reports debated the economic future, after logging, of the northern part of the state. Some writers, like Albert Ellis in *Northern Wisconsin—Its Capacities and Wants* (1852), believed that farming could be successful and that future cities would sprout at the Chippewa settlements at Lac du Flambeau, Lac Vieux Desert, and Lac Courte Oreilles. Others, like the state-sponsored *Geology of Wisconsin* (1873–79), retained some of Owen's original skepticism about agricultural settlement.[7]

The U.S. Geological Survey was one of the first agencies to plan for the post-logging future of the Chippewa River. The U.S.G.S. recognized the potential for a series of flood control dams on the Chippewa River as early as 1879. The most promising site for dam development, it concluded, was on the Chippewa River at the southern boundary of the Lac Courte Oreilles Reservation. The General Land Office also recognized the importance of the Lac Courte Oreilles Reservation in the 1880s when it withdrew from public sale the lands just outside the reservation boundary and to the south of Pahquahwong "for reservoir purposes [although] the Government has constructed no reservoirs yet, nor does it seem likely to. . . ." The Wisconsin Geological and Natural History Survey of 1908 concurred on the value of placing a hydroelectric and flood control dam in southern Sawyer County near Pahquahwong.[8]

The history of the Winter dam site intertwines with the history of riparian rights along the upper Chippewa River Valley. Lumbermen who used the river to drive logs downstream to Chippewa Falls, Eau Claire, and the Mississippi River seasonally altered the river's flow. By 1887, logging firms, especially those associated with Frederick Weyerhaeuser, had constructed almost 150 dams on the upper river and its tributaries in order to release water for the annual log drive. The downriver sawmills also made use of water power to generate their own electricity as early as 1882 at Chippewa Falls. Sufficient electric power was made by falling water in 1898 to open an electric interurban trolley line between Eau Claire and Chippewa Falls.[9] On occasion, the interests of the Weyerhaeuser logging concerns divided the Indians on the LCO Reservation. From the mid-1880's through 1897, the Weyerhaeuser-dominated Chippewa Logging company paid William Billy Boy of LCO for the right to construct a dam on his allotment at the reservation community of Signor. The company employed Billy Boy to maintain the dam during the driving season, and he received an annual rental of $250. At the same time that Billy Boy profited from the use of his property by downstream lumbermen, other Indians at Pahquahwong were upset by a log dam that broke on Pokegama Lake and Pokegama Creek. Some of these residents claimed in May 1894, that the flowage created by the dam had destroyed valuable cranberry marshes and wild rice beds. After the dam broke, "the water continued on our cranberries against our earnest protest," and the Indians calculated that 492 bushels of cranberries had been destroyed and 600 pounds of rice lost, and both crops had been "a great means of sustaining us through the long cold winter just past."[10]

The Weyerhaeuser interests, working through the Chippewa Lumber and Boom Company, decided after the upper river area had been cut-over to sell its dams and riparian rights. The company had logged most of the white pine from the LCO reservation by contract with the Bureau of Indian Affairs, and after the turn of the century, particularly in 1908, severe forest fires had swept the reservation (apparently started by nearby white settlers who used fire to clear their cut-over land). After the decision in 1910 to sell the riparian rights, the company waited until 1912 to sell to pulp-mill developers in Chippewa Falls eager to acquire the rights to generate hydroelectric power. Looking back a decade later, Rudolph Weyerhaeuser wrote from Cloquet, Minnesota, to his brother J. P. Weyerhaeuser that "the biggest mistake we made on the Chippewa was when we let our powers go there. Am satisfied what little water power we have on the St. Louis River will be a valuable asset eventually."[11]

The Chippewa Lumber and Boom Company sold its dam and riparian rights up and down the valley to a new firm called the Chippewa Valley Construction Company, and the new owner in turn sold its rights in Vilas, Oneida, and Sawyer counties to the Chippewa & Flambeau Improvement Company, an outfit founded by other lumbering concerns that sought a means to develop former timber lands. The State of Wisconsin authorized the Chippewa and Flambeau Improvement Company to survey the Pahquahwong site in 1912. The CFI chose a location near Winter, Wisconsin, for the placement of the dam. The resulting flowage would cover 17,000 acres with water, about half of which were within the boundaries of LCO. The Chippewa and Flambeau Improvement Company soon came to work with the Wisconsin-Minnesota Light and Power Company (the outgrowth of the firm that developed the 1898 interurban trolley) to acquire land that would be flooded ("flowage land") if the dam was built. In 1914, the CFI sold its rights to develop the Pahquahwong dam to W-M L & P's parent utility holding company, the American Public Utilities Company of Grand Rapids, Michigan.[12]

American Public Utilities approached the people of Lac Courte Oreilles (LCO) in 1914 and asked them to grant the company the allotted and tribal land around Pahquahwong for the dam. Most of the reservation land slated to be covered by the dam flowage had been allotted to individual Indians, but a few hundred acres belonged to the LCO band itself. The tribal landholding at Lac Courte Oreilles was broken up by individual land allotments, even before the Dawes Act of 1887 made this the federal government's national Indian policy. By the beginning of the twentieth century, much of the tribal land had been sold or lost to whites, through transactions with individual Indians. The company met with a rebuff to its request for either allotted or tribal land, so it decided to bring political pressure to bear on the tribe to concede the desired land. At the national level, American Public Utilities convinced Congress to accede to a change in the reservation's boundary entailed by flooding reservation land, despite the 1854 treaty granting LCO to the Ojibwas in perpetuity. Congress, as part of its Bureau of Indian Affairs authorization in 1916, sanctioned further sales of Lac Courte Oreilles reservation land to developers seeking rights to flowage land. The BIA appropriations act for that year gave the Agency and its parent, the Interior Department, the authority to approve any negotiations and resulting compensation for the sale or lease of flowage lands, whether tribal or consisting of individual allotments. Congress did, however, insist that any land acquired for flowage purposes have the approval of the LCO band. The utility parent also sought to mobilize state politicians to facilitate the dam's development. The state agreed in 1916 to cede state-owned land in the vicinity of LCO to the Ojibwas as new reservation land in turn for cessions at Pahquahwong. The state cessions would then become part of a new LCO, not subject to state taxation.[13]

In the spring of 1916, American Public Utilities sent representatives to LCO to present the Ojibwas with a new proposal to acquire the flowage rights. On January 28, 1916, an official in the company wrote to the superintendent of the Hayward Indian School (the federal official in charge of the LCO Reservation):

> Our Company has the right of eminent domain and I believe it is within our power to obtain by condemnation proceedings the flowage rights on all of the Indian lands which have been allotted to members of the tribe, but we dislike to resort to that expedient

because we feel that the money compensation which would be awarded would not in most cases, no matter how much was awarded, be a fair substitute to the Indians to pay them in other lands to be selected by them, for the flowage rights which we acquire, and if the Indians will negotiate with us on this basis we will make the lands which they receive in exchange for the flowage rights, exempt from taxation, either by obtaining the consent of the State that the lands may be added to the Indian reservation or providing for the payment of taxes so long as the land shall continue to be occupied by the Indians and their descendants.[14]

Negotiations continued during the spring and summer of 1916 between three parties, American Public Utilities, the BIA, and the people of LCO. The company sought to focus the discussion on the acquisition of allotments around Pahquahwong, but agency officials at Hayward realized that "the matter of Indian Tribal Lands . . . may be the crux of the whole question." The company may have enjoyed the right to commence condemnation proceedings on that allotted land, but there was no doubt, as one BIA official put it, that tribal land "is inalienable without the consent of the Indians, [and] they seem to me to be in the position of owners who have found a gold mine on their property and to be entitled to its value."[15]

American Public Utilities came up with a written proposal in the fall of 1916 that it offered the people of LCO and the BIA; the company asked for a public meeting at LCO where it expected that an agreement on the proposal would be reached. The company proposal offered ten concessions to LCO in return for the right to flood tribal land within the reservation boundaries. The key parts of the offer involved acquiring land for a new townsite to relocate the residents from Pahquahwong, along with new houses and new Catholic and Presbyterian churches to replace the ones at The Post. The company also promised to "pay the cost of removing the remains of all deceased Indians, whose graves are in the cemetery at the Post or upon land that will be overflowed. . . ." Additional provisions contained company promises to build highways around the flowage that would connect the new village site to other parts of the Reservation.[16]

The company, the BIA, and the people of LCO came together at a tribal council called by the Hayward School superintendent on November 7, 1916. The superintendent (who served as federal agent for the LCO band from 1908 to 1928) started the council with a greeting and then proceeded to warn the LCO Ojibwas that it was useless to resist the dam:

> This company that is coming here has lots of money behind them and can do anything they say. I have looked for a way to stop this flowage right on your reservation, as I know some of you men do not like to see it come, but I find no way to get around it in the end. I think that in planning to stop this flowage project we are butting our heads against a stone wall. . . . This company has millions of dollars behind them and furnishes electric light for Eau Claire, Chippewa Falls and several other large cities, as well as electric power to drive different machines. This power and light is becoming necessary to take the place of gasoline and wood, which are becoming more scarce year by year, to run the engines and for light. We must not think that the white people do not go ahead and improve the land and settle. They are coming in more each year and taking our game, wild rice and cranberries, and now they want to come in and take electric power on the Pakwewong [sic] lakes. . . . I do not think it would be the best thing for us to try to stop this company for it looks to me too much like butting our heads against a stone wall.[17]

Charles McPherson, the general counsel for the Company, repeated promises made in the company's proposal, and urged the Indians in council to trade the tribal land at The Post for company-provided land on high ground outside the flowage area. After a dinner break in the council, the Indians reconvened and answered McPherson that they would not "consent to make this right," that is, grant the company its wish, and that the tribal members "have no other proposition to make as they had rather have the reservation." McPherson did not take the rejection well and threatened the imminence of "another session of Congress in two months and there is no question but what a law will be passed to give us the Indian village. I am your friend and will continue your friend, but the dam will be built."[18]

Superintendent McQuigg reported the negative decision to his superiors in the BIA in Washington with the comment that the "Indians who did most of the talking are of the more non-progressive and conservative part of the tribe." He later identified them as full-blooded Ojibwas and contrasted their "strong attachment and sentiment to their land which amounts to almost the same thing as fanaticism" with the willingness of mixedbloods living away from Pahquahwong to exchange the tribal land for a better deal. The Superintendent also noted that the older Indians objected to the dam on the basis that it violated the treaty of 1854.[19]

Although McQuigg had sought to pressure the people at LCO into accepting the dam as inevitable, he did faithfully report the anti-dam sentiments of LCO to the BIA Commissioner in Washington. The Bureau sought to head off the company's threat to have Congress pass additional legislation that would condemn tribal as well as allotted land. Commissioner Cato Sells reminded McPherson in July, 1917, that "several councils have been held with the Indians of the reservation and, at least, insofar as the tribal land is concerned, they have as yet failed to give their consent to the granting of such flowage rights."[20]

The company continued its strategy of seeking to acquire flowage rights from the Indian allottees, but it remained stymied on the problem of flooding the tribal land at The Post. In the spring and summer of 1918, the company tried another approach, this time seeking to have the tribal land parcels condemned as a wartime emergency. With the help of the State's Geological and Natural History Survey, the Company approached the U.S. National Council of Defense with the argument that the Pahquahwong dam would save 50,000 to 100,000 tons of coal each year. This strategy of getting around the Indians' opposition to the dam failed only because the war ended in November.

Wisconsin-Minnesota Light & Power Company renewed the ef-

fort in 1919 to obtain tribal permission to flood land on the LCO
Reservation for its dam project. Superintendent McQuigg sought
to avoid a repetition of the earlier tribal council rejections by having the various settlements at LCO elect two delegates apiece to
meet separately with the company. This strategy, too, failed to advance company interests as McQuigg reported, "the delegates are
not willing now to take the responsibility of coming to an agreement and at the councils which were held to elect the delegates no
different propositions have been advanced." McQuigg's heavy-
handedness on the Pahquahwong flowage and other issues, along
with his inability to alleviate some of the reservation misery due
to the influenza epidemic, led the Ojibwas of LCO to demand that
McQuigg be transferred. An investigation by the BIA confirmed
many of the charges and in the winter of 1919, McQuigg ex-
changed places with Robert Craige, the agent at the Turtle Mountain Reservation in North Dakota.[21]

The company sent its representative McPherson to meet with
the tribal council in the spring of 1919 and offered $20,000 in com-
pensation to the tribe for the inundation of about 315 acres of tribal
land. At the same time, the company continued its active acquisition of flowage rights to about 6,000 acres of allotted land that individual Indians owned privately. When the Ojibwas of Lac Courte
Oreilles met once again in tribal council in May, 1919, they rejected
the company offer, as well as another offer to accept land outside
the reservation in compensation. A repeat of the company's offer in
October, 1919 met the same tribal rebuff, this time by a unanimous
vote of the tribe.[22]

The Federal Power Commission and the Dam

With the passage of the Federal Power Act in June, 1920,
Wisconsin-Minnesota Light and Power Company followed yet another tack in its plan to build the Winter Dam. The provisions of the
Federal Power Act gave the new Federal Power Commission the
right to authorize water-power projects on Indian reservations and
on public land. The FPC also had the authority to determine proper

compensation to Indian tribes for the loss of tribal lands to water-power projects. The enabling act provided for public notice and public hearings, but at the same time gave the FPC the direct power to accomplish by administrative ruling what had formerly required an act of Congress. In December of 1920, applying as Project # 108, W-M L & P sought an FPC license to build the Winter Dam, with an anticipated output of 75,000 horsepower. The FPC did seek advice from the Bureau of Indian Affairs over the winter of 1920–21, and the FPC did decide to ask for public comment. The result was a final, tumultuous hearing at Reserve, on the LCO Reservation in May, 1921. The hearing, conducted by the Federal Power Commission, was not held to receive the consent of the band but rather to hear any comments of the Indians before the FPC granted the license with the accompanying power to condemn tribal land.

Superintendent Craige had a sense of strong foreboding when he wrote the commissioner of Indian Affairs for guidance in explaining to LCO residents that the band could no longer withhold its consent to the dam project. "One of the questions that is sure to be presented to me both by the individual allottees and by the tribe in council is 'Is there any authority of law whereby our allotments of tribal land can be condemned for reservoir purposes without our consent?' " Craige also asked for a high official from the BIA in Washington to come to LCO and explain the change in law to the Ojibwas. By 1921, if not earlier, the people of LCO realized that the Bureau of Indian Affairs was unlikely to protect them against either the company or the FPC. Accordingly, the Tribal Business Committee contracted with two private attorneys, E. W. Winton of Madison and Arthur LeSueur of St. Paul.[23]

The May, 1921, general council opened with Superintendent Craige, backed up by an official from the BIA in Washington, spelling out for the Ojibwas the bleak legal situation they faced now that the FPC Act had superseded the 1916 Indian Office appropriations act. He urged them to make a deal with the company before the FPC made its decision, so as to get the most monetary compensation and so "the matter could then be settled under the 1916 law and not the 1920 law." McPherson of the company, also present, repeated his offer of $20,000 or, alternately, 2,000 acres of company-owned land in Sawyer County in exchange for the tribal land as part of an agreement under the 1916 law, but warned "we have been delayed now three or four years . . . if you cannot accept that offer, it is our intention to proceed under the other Act."[24] Several of the Ojibwas at Reserve spoke against the dam after Craige and McPherson had finished their remarks. Majigiwish, who had lived at Pahquahwong by his account "nearly one hundred years," opposed the dam because it would destroy the wild-rice grounds. "I do not depend on flour for to raise my children," he said. "I was almost entirely depending upon the wild Indian rice in raising my children. We have found the Indian rice very beneficial and helpful to us in raising our families. We get the most of our rice right there along the river at the place where this land in question lies."[25] William Wolf, who played a key role as interpreter for the Ojibwas who did not understand English, read a statement that he claimed was the sentiment "of the band as a whole":

> To put under water our sacred bones of our noble forefathers is outrageous. The prayer and desire of this band is to be in the same bosom that shield[s] the remains of our fathers, whenever the time comes. This has been the home of the Ojibways from time unmemorial [sic] and at present there are several Indians in this village, those who are absent are not visiting, but laid beneath the sod of which we call or claim as our home. We have in this village one of the beautiful spots in the reservation and the land is covered by a large tract of small pine which some day the children of the present reservation will enjoy. And further, I the Indian, trusted the Government which is plain in our treaties, to be our guardian and if our guardian consents to the flowage, I will not, I will still hold to my treaty.[26]

The LCO Ojibwas also filed a brief before the FPC contesting the Company's license proposal. Authored by Native American lawyer E. Ward Winton, the brief maintained that the LCO Band opposed the dam on two grounds. First, Winton argued that the FPC Act did not supersede the 1837, 1842, and 1854 treaties, especially the last-named, which guaranteed that "the Indians shall not be required to remove from the homes hereby set apart for them." Winton proceeded to argue that the FPC Act had a provision that reservation land might be flooded only when the dam flowage was not "inconsistent with the purpose for which such reservation was created or acquired." Winton insisted that the dam's construction went beyond mere interference; indeed, the purpose of the reservation would be "entirely destroyed if the license [were] issued and the lands flooded."[27]

Consisting of the secretaries of War, Interior, and Agriculture and an executive staff, the FPC was clearly inclined to grant the Company its license even before the Reserve hearing and before receiving Winton's brief. O. C. Merrill, the Executive Secretary to the FPC, asked the BIA Commissioner "that action on this case be expedited. The project appears to be a desirable one, and the applicant is anxious to start work this season." The only question that Merrill thought needed resolution was the amount of compensation due the LCO Ojibwas.[28]

Despite the opposition from Indians at Lac Courte Oreilles, the FPC (with support from the Bureau of Indian Affairs) granted a fifty-year license to W-M L & P to construct and operate the dam on August 8, 1921, and work commenced the next year. The license provided for the building of an earth-filled dam nearly one thousand feet long and forty-five feet high, with the goal of creating a reservoir thirty-five feet higher than the river's old water level. The dam was completed in 1923 and when the gates were closed in March of that year, Wisconsin suddenly had a lake known as the "Chippewa Flowage," also known as "Lake Chippewa," covering 17,000 acres, bigger than all but two of the state's other 9,000 or so lakes. Of the acreage submerged under the Chippewa Flowage, about 8,000 acres was land obtained from within the 1854 boundaries of the Lac Courte Oreilles Reservation, though by 1921 not all of this land was still under tribal or individual Indian control. In the case of the Winter Dam and Chippewa Flowage, the FPC directed W-M L & P to pay an annual lease of $1,200, which was six percent of the $20,000 that the Indians had rejected in 1919 as compensation for flooded tribal land; furthermore, as matters turned out, the Chippewa Flowage actually inundated 525 acres of tribal land, not the envisioned 315, and, therefore, in the 1930s, the FPC ordered the Northern States Power Company (by then, the dam's operator) to pay an additional annual charge.[29]

Before the Winter Dam created the Chippewa Flowage, the Wisconsin-Minnesota Light and Power Company agreed to move some of the buildings of a threatened Indian settlement known as "The Post" to a new location, soon dubbed "New Post." Moreover, the company promised to disinter the remains of known Indian graves around The Post for reburial on dry ground. The company's performance of these obligations, however, fell short of what had been promised in 1921 in nearly every aspect; the most shocking breach of the license was the company's failure to disinter nearly two centuries of Indians buried in the path of the flowage. For the next fifty years, various gravesites of Indians were exposed above water in the winter when the dam operators drew the water level down for purposes of power generation and flood control.[30]

Wisconsin-Minnesota Light & Power reorganized in the 1920s as Northern States Power Company, and that utility operated the Winter Dam over the length of the FPC license. In 1971, NSP applied for another fifty-year license from the FPC. Opposition to renewal came from an alliance of Lac Court Oreilles Indians who wished to regain control of the land under, around and actually in (i.e., islands) the artificial Chippewa Flowage, and environmental groups who objected to NSP's flood-control technique of annually drawing down the Flowage with a resulting damage to the neighboring wetlands and lake fish. An unintended consequence of the W-M L & P dam and flowage was the creation of a sportsperson's treasure in the 1920s that produced some of the finest sport fishing in the United States. Some of Wisconsin's congressional delegation sided with the opponents of NSP, though the threatened loss of tax revenue from NSP caused most of the local government bodies to rally around the power company. LCO Indians made the most dramatic protest in 1971 by occupying the dam site as part of the "Red Power" movement that was active nationwide, and the tribe launched a lawsuit against NSP for damages over the entire history of the Chippewa Flowage project, a legal action that lasted well into the 1980s.

In 1985, the Lac Courte Oreilles band and NSP settled their legal differences. The band took over operation of the dam and built its own electric generating plant on the site. The band worked with the state Department of Natural Resources to protect fish population in the Chippewa Flowage by controlling the water level. The LCO band also agreed to work with NSP in controlling the release of water to avoid downstream floods. NSP also transferred 4,500 acres of company-owned land to the band, including 2,300 acres situated within the 1854 treaty boundary of the reservation. Finally, NSP made a monetary settlement with the band to compensate for past damages and legal expenses.[31]

The Dam in Historical Perspective

We are far enough removed from the events of 1921, and perhaps the events of 1971 as well, to gain a little historical perspective. We can review the various historical actors between 1900 and 1921. A critical, if somewhat distant player was the federal government, though it is important to note that it was represented by several agencies with conflicting directives and imperatives. The U.S. Geological Service initiated the formal planning of the Winter Dam with its 1879 survey of the flood control and power potential of the Upper Chippewa River. The Bureau of Indian Affairs had been dealing with the Ojibwa Indians, including the Lac Courte Oreilles band, since the Jacksonian Era. The BIA's responsibilities expanded considerably in the 1880s as official government policy for all American Indians was one that discouraged tribalism and encouraged individual agricultural enterprise. The key federal entity in the history of the Winter Dam was the Federal Power Commission, a new agency established in 1920, that had the specific mandate to develop the nation's hydroelectric power potential. Staffed by federal personnel on detail from the War, Interior and Agriculture Departments, the FPC in the aftermath of World War I faced an avalanche of applications for permission to use waterways for power development.[32]

The State of Wisconsin, through its various agencies had also expressed an interest in the resources of the upper Chippewa. In 1906, the State Forester reported to the governor and legislature that "the development of the water powers of Wisconsin is in its infancy and as the lumber industry dies out and we look more and more to manufacturing, all water powers, large and small, will become increasingly valuable and the necessity of protecting them more apparent." The State Forester also argued that the state had an interest in the riparian rights of northern Wisconsin rivers because "it is very unwise to allow a few companies owning dams to thus virtually control all the water powers on any river."[33]

The State Commissioner of Fisheries in the first decade of the twentieth century was quite concerned with northern Wisconsin rivers and lakes for a different type of economic development. "While these inland waters have a local importance as yielding food," the 1908 report maintained, "their value as a means of sport and recreation is much greater, both to the state and to the community in which the lake is situated." Two years later, the fish commissioner foresaw a future in which numerous people "who will spend their summers in Wisconsin in pursuit of health [and] recreation, and the chief incentive will be to catch the fish that abound in our thousands of inland lakes and streams."[34]

The Geological and Natural History Survey showed its interest in 1908, though its flood-control concerns weighed as heavily as those involving hydroelectric power development. The Chippewa River had flooded downstream towns and cities throughout the late nineteenth century, and some sort of flood control seemed desirable to the state. The state legislature sought to help the proposed dam and flowage along in 1917 by offering to exchange state lands to the LCO Chippewa in return for land lost to flowage flooding.[35]

The Chippewa River between the 1850s and the 1890s had been the principal highway of commerce in the American white pine logging industry. Tens of billions of board feet of lumber had been cut by the end of the nineteenth century and floated down the Chippewa River to the sawmills of Chippewa Falls and Eau Claire, and down the Mississippi to the Quad Cities or Hannibal and St. Louis. The dominant firm that emerged out of the competitive struggle for control of the Chippewa was Frederick Weyerhaeuser's Chippewa Log and Boom Company. By 1910, nearly all of the original forest of northern Wisconsin had been logged, and the lumber companies controlled by men such as Weyerhaeuser faced a problem of what to do with their "cut-over" land. They simply abandoned some land for taxes, but many of the lumber companies sought to attract prospective farmers to northern Wisconsin to transform the former pineries into a productive agricultural region. The Chippewa and Flambeau Improvement Company was one such company involved in trying to alter the land use of the upper Chippewa Valley.[36]

The most ambitious project planned and constructed along the entire 300-mile Chippewa River, the Winter Dam was the farthest away from population centers. The goal of the Wisconsin-Minnesota Light and Power Company was to use the dam at Winter primarily for the purpose of controlling the flow of river water so as to maximize the power generating capability of company hydro plants at four sites from fifty to one hundred miles downstream. In 1917 it constructed a high-voltage transmission line to supply the growing population center of Minneapolis and St. Paul. Long-distance transmission was thereafter a company goal, not just the creation of abundant cheap power for local economic development, although, later in the 1920s, the growing industrial city of Eau Claire did come to absorb all the hydro power that NSP could generate.[37]

The final and most compelling historical actor in the history of the Winter Dam was the band of Lac Courte Oreilles Ojibwa Indians. By the time of the final deliberations over the dam, they had endured forty years of federal policy designed to transform their complex and collective tribal economy of hunting, fishing, gathering and gardening into a set of farmers working individual allotments. Several years before the Dawes Act of 1887, Congress had decreed that the Lac Courte Oreilles Reservation be broken up into individual allotments with men, women, and children getting different acreages. Congress allowed the sale of these allotments after 1901 with results similar to those on other reservations across the continent: whites came to acquire a significant portion of the reservation land. Moreover, Indians at Lac Courte Oreilles had lost a considerable part of their timber due to illegal depredations.[38]

The actors in the history of the Winter Dam need to be understood in the terms of their own times and places. If, using the typology developed by Wisconsin's own Frederick Jackson Turner, one had to place northern Wisconsin in a specific historical period in 1921, it would be the "post-frontier" stage. With the receding of the lumber frontier, the region's history entered its next phase, one of manufacturing, farming, and, later, tourism. Contemporaries understood this, most notably the State Geologist who maintained in 1908 that the Chippewa River could most profitably be devoted to power generation now that its duty had been done as a transporter of logs.[39]

The specific actors also should be placed within the histories of their agencies or corporate environments. The FPC came at the end of the Progressive Era, which had been twenty years of uneasy cooperation in regulation and development between private enterprise and the federal government. The same could be said for the State of Wisconsin, which had forcefully used state agencies to promote economic development, a concept known then as the "Wisconsin Idea." On the private enterprise side, Wisconsin-Minnesota Light & Power Company was in the midst of inventing a regional generating and transmission system, one that, like California's, used distant upland falling water to produce electricity for a metropolis. In a certain sense, W-M L and P entertained a broad view of the Chippewa Valley, arguing that the particular local interests of the Indians had to give way before the greater interests of the entire valley, and indeed, the entire upper Mississippi region. This viewpoint proved quite persuasive with all but the Indians. The FPC had little doubt about the national benefits of Project #108, and in intra-governmental dealings, it convinced the Bureau of Indian Affairs, too.[40]

The reported unanimity of opposition to the Winter Dam by the Lac Courte Oreilles band of Chippewa Indians deserves some additional comment. Their history also needs to be set within the context of several centuries of dealing with Europeans and their descendents. The Lac Courte Oreilles contained among them a significant number of Indians of mixed French and Chippewa descent, a people in other times and places known as *métis* or, in the English of the time, as "mixed-bloods," or, disparagingly, as "half-breeds." About the same time that Lac Courte Oreilles Reservation was beset by the problem of the Winter Dam, the large neighboring Chippewa reservation at White Earth in Minnesota was torn by factionalism between a group who claimed to be "full blood" and a minority of enterprising land acquirers accused of being "French" or "mixed-blood." At White Earth, the struggle was over whether to accept the BIA push to become individual farmers or to seek to maintain a tribal, communal economy. The "mixed-bloods" sought an accommodation with the BIA plan and, since they were the traditional traders of the band, they also had something of an advantage in a competitive environment of acquisition and gain. There are hints of something of the same struggle at Lac Courte Oreilles in the years up to World War I, yet the Winter Dam served to unite the tribe in 1921, not divide it as one might imagine. Perhaps the Winter Dam proposal was so overwhelming, the insult to the tribe so obnoxious, and the proposed payment so puny that even those Chippewa Indians disposed towards aggressive individual capital acquisition saw their future threatened by the giant dam and flowage. After the Chippewa Flowage filled with water, the reservation community at LCO was physically split by the water. Communication was made more difficult between the principal LCO villages of Reserve and New Post.[41]

The summer of 1921 revealed three attitudes toward economic organization on the upper Chippewa River. At one end was the vision of Wisconsin-Minnesota Light and Power, along with the FPC and the State of Wisconsin, which thought of regional flood control for the Chippewa Valley, and the expanding electricity demand of the Twin Cities of Minneapolis and St. Paul. This involved joint private and public development of distant water resources such as the site on the upper Chippewa above Winter at Pahquahwong. A second approach to economic organization was that of the Bureau of

Indian Affairs, as represented through its agent to the Ojibwa in Wisconsin, and through the commissioner's office in Washington. The BIA still advocated a Jeffersonian farmer's life to Indians at LCO, and, while it agreed with the FPC about the nominal importance of Project #108, it also wished to discourage the Ojibwa Indians from traditional hunting and gathering on the reservation. There was also the united attitude of the tribe that the dam and flowage threatened its communal economy of hunting, fishing, and wild-rice gathering. Moreover, the flowage would inundate one of the two main hamlets on the reservation and require disturbing the burial sites of the dead. No price paid in dollars by W-M P & L, nor any argument about the benefits downstream in terms of flood control or power to the Twin Cities could convince the Ojibwas that the dam should be supported. Nearly seven decades later, there is a strong feeling among the LCO Ojibwas that what took place in 1921 and after was truly the crime of the century. For more than half a century the people of LCO had lost control over the land within their reservation. Upon regaining control of the Flowage, the dam site, and the NSP acreage, the tribal chief—himself a descendant of the villagers at the Old Post—commented, "Justice seems to take forever."[42]

JAMES W. OBERLY has been an expert witness on behalf of Wisconsin Ojibwa bands in treaty-rights litigation. He received the doctorate from the University of Rochester and has taught on a number of Indian reservations. His research interests include the application of computer-assisted methodology to American Indian ethnohistory. Kent State University Press published his book, *Sixty Million Acres: American Veterans and the Public Lands before the Civil War.*

Notes

1. See Patricia Nelson Limerick, *The Legacy of Conquest: The Unbroken Past of the American West* (New York, 1987); Michael L. Lawson, *Damned Indians: The Pick-Sloan Plan and the Missouri River Sioux, 1944–1980* (Norman, Oklahoma, 1982); Richard White, *The Roots of Dependency: Subsistence, Environment, and Social Change among the Choctaws, Pawnees, and Navajos* (Lincoln, Nebraska, 1983); and Ronald N. Satz, *Chippewa Treaty Rights: The Reserved Rights of Wisconsin's Chippewa Indians in Historical Perspective* (Madison, 1991).

2. A good introduction to the history of the Winter Dam and Chippewa Flowage project is the report of the Inland Lakes Demonstration Project, *Chippewa Flowage Investigations* (Madison, 1972), especially volume 3A, appendices H and L.

3. William Warren, *History of the Ojibway* (New York, 1885); Edmund J. Danziger, Jr., *The Chippewas of Lake Superior* (Norman, Oklahoma, 1978); Donald Fixico, "Chippewa Fishing and Hunting Rights and the Voight Decision," in *An Anthology of Western Great Lakes Indian History*, edited by Donald Fixico (Milwaukee, 1987), 481–521; "Disbursal of Lac Court Oreilles Band Trust Funds," Hearing before the Senate Select Committee on Indian Affairs, 97th Congress, 1st Session (Washington, 1981), 46; Satz, *Chippewa Treaty Rights*, chapter 2.

4. Frances Densmore, "Uses of Plants by the Chippewa Indians," *Forty-fourth Annual Report of the Bureau of American Ethnology* (Washington, 1926–27), 286–94; Daniel Bushnell (Sub-Agent) to Commissioner of the Indian Office, Sept. 30, 1840, in Letters Received from the La Pointe Agency, Records of the Bureau of Indian Affairs, Record Group 75, National Archives and Records Administration, Microfilm Series 234, Roll 388; David Dale Owen, *Report of a Geological Survey of Wisconsin, Iowa, and Minnesota* (Philadelphia, 1852), 280–81.

5. See the 1863 correspondence generated by Agent L. E. Webb in Letters Received from the La Pointe Agency (cited above), Roll 394, frames 106 and 119.

6. *Biennial Report of the Commissioner of State Forests* (Madison, 1906), 22–24. The Forest Commissioner also did a study analyzing the causes of forty-two forest fires that blazed in the northern counties in 1906. Twenty-one were set by settlers clearing land, seven by hunters searching

for game, twelve by unknown persons, and two by Indians. See page 17 of
the report cited above.

7. Owen, xxii, 148–49; Albert Ellis, *Northern Wisconsin—Its Capacities and Wants* (Madison, 1852).

8. *Annual Report of Commissioner of the General Land Office* (Washington, 1881), 78.

9. A list of logging dams on the upper Chippewa River may be found in
the Kohlmeyer Papers, Box 2, "Riparian Rights" folder, Forest History Society, Duke University.

10. To the Commissioner of Indian Affairs, May 23, 1894, in Letters
Received from the Lac Court Oreilles Agency, Record Group 75, Records of
the Bureau of Indian Affairs, National Archives and Records Administration, Great Lakes Region (Federal Records Center, Chicago).

11. Randolph Weyerhaeuser to J. P. Weyerhauser, March 27, 1922, in
Kohlmeyer Papers, Box 2, "Riparian Rights" folder, Forest History Society.

12. Chief Engineer of the U.S. Army, *Annual Report* (Washington,
1880), 1648; Wisconsin Geological and Natural History Survey, *The Water
Powers of Wisconsin* (Madison, 1908), 181–206; *Chippewa Flowage Investigations*, volume 3A, pp. H1–H5; and Kohlmeyer Papers, Box 2, "Riparian
Rights" folder, Forest History Society.

13. U.S., *Statutes at Large*, volume 39, pp. 123–59; *Chippewa Flowage
Investigations*, volume 3A, pp. L46–L48.

14. Charles McPherson to Superintendent of Hayward Indian School,
Jan. 28, 1916. This and the subsequent citations to specific correspondence items and minutes are taken from the series "Letters Received from the Hayward School and Agency, 1908–1928," Record Group
75, Records of the Bureau of Indian Affairs, National Archives and
Records Administration, Great Lakes Region (Federal Records Center,
Chicago).

15. Hayward Superintendent to Commissioner of Indian Affairs, Nov.
14, 1916.

16. American Public Utilities Company "Proposition" (1916).

17. Minutes of the Tribal Council, Nov. 7, 1916, pp. 1–3.

18. Minutes of the Tribal Council, Nov. 7, 1916, p. 5.

19. Minutes of the Tribal Council, Nov. 7, 1916, pp. 6–7.

20. Commissioner of Indian Affairs to Charles McPherson, July 3, 1917.

21. Superintendent of Hayward School to Commissioner of Indian Af-

fairs, Jan. 16, 1919; and Superintendent of Hayward School to Phillip Gordon, Aug. 21, 1919.

22. *Chippewa Flowage Investigations,* volume 3A, pp. H1–H5.

23. Superintendent of Hayward School to Commissioner of Indian Affairs, April 15, 1921; Eldon Marple, *The Visitor Who Came to Stay: Legacy of the Hayward Area* (Hayward, 1971), 46–52.

24. Minutes of the Tribal Council, May 17, 1921.

25. Minutes of the Tribal Council, May 17, 1921. See also Thomas Vennum, Jr., *Wild Rice and the Ojibway People* (St. Paul, 1988), 294.

26. Minutes of the Tribal Council, May 17, 1921.

27. E. W. Winton, "Brief Reply to Brief for Applicant" (1921).

28. O. C. Merrill to Commissioner of Indian Affairs, April 15, 1921.

29. *Chippewa Flowage Investigations,* volume 3A, pp. L48–L53.

30. Project #108, Federal Power Commission License (Aug. 8, 1921), articles 14 and 15; Marple, *The Visitor Who Came to Stay,* 52.

31. *Chippewa Flowage Investigations,* volume 3A, pp. H22–H24. Joe Wilson, "The Restoration of the Lac Court Oreilles Indians' Lost Land: The Controversy over the Relicensing of the Lac Court Oreilles Hydroelectric Dam from 1971 to 1987," in *Studies in Wisconsin's Native American History: An Anthology of Undergraduate Research,* edited by James Oberly. (Eau Claire: University of Wisconsin–Eau Claire, 1990), 309–11.

32. Milton Conover, *The Federal Power Commission* (Baltimore, 1923); Paul Stuart, *The Indian Office: Growth and Development of an American Institution, 1865–1900* (Ann Arbor, 1979).

33. *Biennial Report of the Commissioner of State Forests,* 1906, 28–29.

34. *Biennial Report of the Commissioner of Fisheries* (Madison, 1908), 13; *Biennial Report of the Commissioner of Fisheries* (Madison, 1910), 27.

35. *The Water Powers of Wisconsin,* 205.

36. Ralph W. Hidy, *Timber and Men: The Weyerhaeuser Story* (New York, 1963); Charles Twining, *Downriver: Orrin H. Ingram and the Empire Lumber Company* (Madison, 1975).

37. Herbert W. Meyer, *Builders of Northern States Power Company* (Minneapolis, 1957), 107–22.

38. Nancy O. Lurie, *Wisconsin Indians* (Madison, 1987); see also "Condition of Indian Affairs in Wisconsin," Hearings before the Senate Committee on Indian Affairs, 60th Congress, 1st Session (Washington, 1910), 126–95.

39. Frederick Jackson Turner, *The Frontier in American History* (New York, 1920); *Water Powers of Wisconsin*, 200–206.

40. Thomas P. Hughes, *Networks of Power: Electrification in Western Society, 1880–1930* (Baltimore, 1983), chapter 10; Stanley Lebergott, *The Americans: An Economic Record* (New York, 1985), 351–56.

41. Melissa Meyer, "Warehousers and Sharks: Chippewa Leadership and Political Factionalism on the White Earth Reservation, 1907–1920," in Fixico, *Anthology*, 407–36; and Meyer, "Signatures and Thumbprints: Ethnicity among the White Earth Anishinaabeg," *Social Science History* 14 (Fall, 1990): 305–45; *Chippewa Flowage Investigations*, pp. H8–H9.

42. Wilson, "The Restoration of the Lac Court Oreilles Indians' Lost Land," 316.

Suggestions for Further Reading

Dawson, Michael L. *Dammed Indians: The Pick-Sloan Plan and the Missouri River Sioux, 1944–1980.* Norman: University of Oklahoma Press, 1980.

Densmore, Frances. *Chippewa Customs.* St. Paul: Minnesota Historical Society Press, 1979, Reprint of 1929 edition (U.S. Government Printing Office, Washington, DC).

Helgeson, Arlan. *Farms in the Cutover: Agricultural Settlement in Northern Wisconsin.* Madison: State Historical Society of Wisconsin, 1962.

Hidy, Ralph Willard. *Timber and Men: The Wyerhaeuser Story.* New York: Macmillan, 1963.

Hoxie, Frederick. *A Final Promise: The Campaign to Assimilate the Indians, 1880–1920.* Lincoln: University of Nebraska Press, 1984.

Hughes, Thomas P. *Networks of Power: Electrification in Western Society, 1880–1930.* Baltimore: Johns Hopkins University Press, 1983.

Inland Lakes Demonstration Project. *Chippewa Flowage Investigation Conducted with Regard to Relicensing of Federal Power Commission Project #108.* Madison: Wisconsin Department of Natural Resources, 1972.

Lurie, Nancy O. *Wisconsin Indians.* Madison: State Historical Society of Wisconsin, 1987.

Meyer, Herbert W. *Builders of Northern States Power Company.* Minneapolis: Northern States Power Company, 1957.

Meyer, Melissa L. *The White Earth Tragedy: Ethnicity and Dispossession at a Minnesota Anishinaabe Reservation, 1889–1920.* Lincoln: University of Nebraska Press, 1994.

Satz, Ronald N. *Chippewa Treaty Rights: The Reserved Rights of the Chippewa Indians in Historical Perspective.* Madison: Wisconsin Academy of Sciences, Arts and Letters, 1991.

Blackbird Women

Denise Sweet

University of Wisconsin–Green Bay

I t was Aunt Gen who first raised my suspicions about the Sisters at Our Lady of Lourdes. Like at my first communion. She heard one of the Sisters say, "I think of the children as my very own." Aunt Gen about had a fit when she heard that one. We had to leave in a hurry. She said to me on the way back to White Earth in Uncle Cece's truck, "They got their eyes on you, my girl." She was looking out the window at the time.

Aunt Gen and my mom don't see eye to eye about the Sisters. My Aunt Gen thinks like the old-timers on our reservation think and she don't like the parish school or the Sisters or nothing. "We're no match against that medicine of theirs," Aunt Gen says. "Look at us—our kids making signs across and forgetting about Winabojo. Grownups ashamed of old Indi'n ways."

My mom thinks parish school is the greatest thing since indoor toilets. She don't want me to go to no school that don't teach catechism. My Uncle Cece works at the sawmill in Winston so he drops me and my stupid brother off every morning at the school. I don't like the ride very much. Sometimes I get sick to my stomach and have to eat soda crackers. Uncle Cece keeps some in the glove box for me.

My mom don't want Aunt Gen to talk about witches to me either, but it don't matter. I'm only eleven but I've known for a long time about some people having powers and some not. Take me for example. I'm left-handed and my father was a full-blood. I was also born with pierced ears. All the old-timers came to see the baby who was born with pierced ears, Aunt Gen told me. Sometimes you're born lucky. But you have to be careful. Aunt Gen says not to brag or your magic will turn on you or something will take it from you. So I'm careful, especially around the Sisters. They are all witches for sure, says Aunt Gen.

I've been thinking about the Sisters at Our Lady of Lourdes like they may be up to no good with me. For one thing, they try to make me write with my right hand when I do much nicer with my left. Aunt Gen says forcing someone to go against their natural direction is like trying to change the flow of a river. Uncle Cece says the Anglos can do that too.

And then there was the hair note I brung home last winter. Sister Stephanie's in charge of dress and personal grooming and one day she sent a note home with me. The note said Sister Stephanie found a creepy-crawler in my hair. It said the long hair had to go. My mom was so ashamed. I told her not to worry. Since the nights had been so cold, Makwa, that fleabag dog of ours had been crawling into my bed. That's where the bugs came from. My mom got over it, but she told me not to tell anyone about this. That made me mad. I wanted to tell my friends Jerry Hokanen and Patrick O'Grintz. Neither of them have dogs, much less creepy-crawlers.

When Aunt Gen saw my hair cut short, whoa was she mad! She let out a howl that sent Makwa barrelling through the kitchen, scratching at the door to go outside. Uncle Cece don't say too much, but he started yelling at Aunt Gen this time. He told her to sit down and listen while my mom explained. My mom seemed like she was expecting this kind of reaction from Aunt Gen. She told her my hair would grow back in time and besides short hair looked nice on me. It was no good. Hair is a big thing to Aunt Gen. When Aunt Gen looks at me now, she has this way of looking as though something was hovering over the top of my head. Makes her look as though she's bit a wormy apple. I don't know what it is. I'd never had a haircut before. The ends of my hair feel sharp and bristly. I do sort of miss my braid.

After the hair note, Aunt Gen started sitting me down and talking to me about those old blackbirds at Our Lady of Lourdes. Mostly she warns me not to believe everything the Sisters tell me especially when it comes to sinful acts. She also talks to me about the prayers. Aunt Gen says it just isn't a good idea to be a nag to the Creator about how bad you think you are and how bad you'll always be. To her, this is like bragging. Besides, calling for help all the time with only yourself in mind is false reverence, Aunt Gen says. Being grateful and giving thanks, now that's a different story. Keep your prayers for special, she tells me.

Here's where word-songs come in handy. I say these for my own amusement during Mass or while I'm waiting for confession. Here's one I say instead of Our Father. You can use it, but if you say it outloud and catch heck, I'll deny I ever heard of such a thing:

Cow fodder, warts and seven
tallow plugs your brain,
thy king is dumb,
thy rope is rung,
an earthworm's in your navel.

Give us a dog to dunk our bread,
and fleabag our best guests,
as we fleabag those
who pass gas against us.

Now you are shabby, and what a wide end (sometimes I whistle here)
amen. way ah hey hey

One night at bedtime prayers, I started my favorite "half monkey, full of grapes," and my mom was standing in the hallway and overheard me. I do believe she thrashed me within an inch of my life. She don't think that kind of thing is very funny. I'm more careful now.

At school, Patrick O'Grintz and Jerry Hokenen and I have this special club for witch-hunting. Like Aunt Gen says, you got to be on your guard and we're just the ones to do it. We keep watch over all the kids, especially the ones who play by themselves. See, when you're alone a lot, it's easy for a witch to raise heck with you.

Our second duty is to spy on the Sisters. This is the best part of being a witchhunter. During recess Jerry Hokanen, Patrick O'Grintz and I hide under the stairwell next to the Sisters' meeting room and wait for the last one of them to go in. When she shuts the door, we move in and listen for witch plans.

Sometimes it's hard to tell witch plans from teacher plans. Patrick said the Sisters probably use a code language and we would have to break the master code to understand what's going on. It was his idea to put our songbooks for High Mass up to a mirror, but we deciphered nothing. Latin is Latin, even backwards in a mirror. But Patrick has not given up. He is good at this kind of thing. He's left-handed too.

Well, we've been listening for a couple of days straight and nothing has come of it. We're under the stairwell again and Jerry's telling about Nancy Lanari talking right outloud during her confession last Thursday when we hear this terrible rumbling up above us. It sounds as though someone has fallen the whole flight of stairs, head over teakettles. I don't dare move. I'm so scared of being found in the building during recess time that I can hear my own heart beating inside my skull. Then we hear someone say "goddammit" and really mean it. It was Sister Adelbert.

And then Patrick O'Grintz starts giggling. Patrick is my best friend and all, but he can't control himself very well. I want to see Sister Adelbert laid out on the floor as much as anyone, rubbing her fanny and cussing like my Uncle Cece, but laughing at the Sisters is inviting trouble. We were supposed to be out on the playground.

Patrick holds his breath and I pinch his nose but it don't help. He's hopeless. Next thing I know, he's cracking up, right outloud, and Jerry Hokanen can't help but laugh with him. I'm so mad at them both, I feel like crying.

It's too late. Sister Adelbert picks herself up off the floor and comes over to where we were hiding. The witchhunters of Our Lady of Lourdes have been found. Sister is so mad to see us inside during recess that her face is all white and puffed up like the underbelly of a catfish. The hair note was nothing compared to the note that was to come out of this.

Sister Adelbert was a whole lot stronger than any of us ever gave her credit for. She grabs me by one arm and lifts me up and out from under the stairwell like I was some scrawny chicken about to be butchered. She does the same to Patrick and Jerry until the three of us are standing in a row in front of her, wishing we had the magic enough to disappear into thin air.

She marches us up to fourth floor to see the principal, Sister Ignatia. I thought I saw her once at a school picnic. Sister Ignatia's got to be the skinniest nun I've ever seen. That stiff white habit sort of cuts into her forehead and her cheekbones stick out like chunks of ice. Her hands look like claws and her glasses set on the tip of her peaked nose, steaming up with every squawk that comes from her paper-thin lips. That day at the picnic, Sister Ignatia had been standing at the top of the stairs outside in front of the school, like some old scarecrow with her long black habit flapping around her legs. One of the eighth-grade boys said that one time the wind had whipped her habit high enough so's you could see she wore long johns, but I never believed it. In the middle of May?

Sister Ignatia whispers something to Sister Adelbert, and the next thing I know, I'm watching Jerry and Patrick walk away from me with Sister Adelbert holding the door for them. I try to follow, but Sister Ignatia steps in my way and closes the door behind them. I look around her office, trying to avoid her eyes. I remember Aunt Gen saying that if you lock gazes with a witch, they can steal your thoughts. This I didn't need. I look out the window at the playground and try to watch some kids play crack the whip.

Then Sister Ignatia tells me to go to the cupboard near the closet in her office. I'm to bring her the jar of beans. I open the cupboard and haul out a jar of black turtle beans and place them on her desk. She opens the jar and tells me to scatter them in a row on the floor. By now, I'm getting pretty scared. What sort of magic is this? Aunt Gen never told me about beans, only that they're good in soup. Corn, butternut squash and black turtle beans. She calls it Three Sisters Soup.

Sister Ignatia wants me to kneel on the beans. I don't believe her at first. She says I'm harder to train than the others and that I have relatives who consort with the devil. She presses me to the floor and my knees settle into the hard black plugs. My knees begin to hurt so bad that I know for certain I will die from this penance. Sister Ignatia hands me her rosary and stands over me, holding the back of my neck. We begin. For the first time in my life, I say an Our Father as though I am a sinner. When Aunt Gen heard of my punishment, she made Uncle Cece drive her to parish school to see Sister Ignatia. She came home and told my mom she was going to keep me away from those cussed blackbirds at the school. My mom just stood there and listened while Aunt Gen told her what they did to me. Aunt Gen made me go to my room. I try to listen but Makwa tries to scratch open my door and starts to whine. I can hear Aunt Gen and Uncle Cece talk Indian about what has happened.

Makwa pushes the door open and jumps on my bed. I am trying to study my catechism because tomorrow there will be a quiz on the Holy Days of Obligation. Aunt Gen brings me a cup of tea and sits on the bed to watch me drink it. She doesn't say anything for a long time. Then she takes a tiny bundle of cedar that she has made and puts it in between my blankets like she was tucking a little kitten away to sleep. Aunt Gen says that that old witch is afraid. We have a strong medicine, she says and shakes her fist. All I want to know is why Sister Ignatia punished me and not Patrick or Jerry. But I don't ask Aunt Gen. I want to tell her that she was right. Sister Ignatia is sure enough an old witch blackbird with a magic stronger than anything I can muster. But it's hard to make the words come. Any magic left in me, I'd better save pretty much just to stay alive.

DENISE SWEET teaches poetry, creative writing, and American Indian literature at the University of Wisconsin–Green Bay. Her work has appeared in *Calyx, Upriver, Plainswoman, Political Palate, Transactions: Journal of the Wisconsin Academy of Sciences, Arts and Letters, Sinister Wisdom,* and *Women Brave in the Face of Danger: Photographs and Writings by Latin and North American Women.* In 1985, Denise received one of the awards for Outstanding Indian Women, presented by the Positive Indian Development Center and the Wisconsin Women's Council. She is a member of the Minnesota Chippewa Tribe, enrolled at White Earth Reservation.

Suggestions for Further Reading

Allen, Paula Gunn. *The Woman Who Owned the Shadows.* San Francisco: Spinsters/Aunt Lute Book Company, 1983.

Bataille, Gretchen M. *American Indian Women: A Guide to Research.* New York: Garland, 1991.

Bataille, Gretchen M. *American Indian Women: Telling Their Lives.* Lincoln: University of Nebraska Press, 1984.

Broker, Ignatia. *Night Flying Women.* St. Paul: Minnesota Historical Society Press, 1983.

Bruchac, Joseph. *Keepers of the Animals: Native American Stories and Wildlife Activities for Children.* Golden, CO: Fulcrum, 1991.

Bruchac, Joseph. *Native American Animal Stories.* Golden, CO: Fulcrum, 1992.

Bruchac, Joseph. *Native American Stories.* Golden, CO: Fulcrum, 1991.

Bruchac, Joseph. *Thirteen Moons on Turtle's Back: A Native American Year of Moons.* New York: Philomel, 1992.

Crow Dog, Mary, and Richard Erdoes. *Lakota Woman.* New York: Grove-Weidenfeld, 1990.

Dorris, Michael. *A Yellow Raft in Blue Water.* New York: Henry Holt, 1987.

Erdrich, Louise. *The Beet Queen: A Novel.* New York: Holt, 1986.

Erdrich, Louise. *The Bingo Palace.* New York: HarperCollins, 1994.

Erdrich, Louise. *Tracks.* New York: Harper and Row, 1988.

Green, Rayna. *That's What She Said: Contemporary Poetry and Fiction by Native American Women.* Bloomington: Indiana University Press, 1984.

Hobson, Geary, ed. *The Remembered Earth: An Anthology of Contemporary Native American Literature.* Albuquerque, NM: Red Earth Press, 1979.

Johnston, Basil. *Ojibway Heritage.* Lincoln/London: University of Nebraska Press, 1990.

Johnston, Basil. *Ojibway Tales.* Lincoln/London: University of Nebraska Press, 1978.

Lurie, Nancy O., ed. *Mountain Wolf Woman, Sister of Crashing Thunder: The Autobiography of a Winnebago Woman.* Ann Arbor: University of Michigan Press, 1961.

Momaday, N. Scott. *House Made of Dawn.* New York: Perennial, 1990.

Momaday, N. Scott. "The Man Made of Words." In *Indian Voices: First Convocation of American Indian Scholars.* San Francisco: Indian Historian Press, 1970.

Momaday, N. Scott. *The Names: A Memoir.* New York: Harper and Row, 1976.

Momaday, N. Scott. *The Way to Rainy Mountain.* Albuquerque: University of New Mexico Press, 1964.

Niatum, Duane, ed. *Harper's Anthology of 20th Century Native American Poetry.* San Francisco: Harper and Row, 1988.

Sweet, Denise. *Know by Heart.* Eau Claire, WI: Rhiannon Press, 1992.

Vizenor, Gerald. *The People Named the Chippewa: Narrative Histories.* Minneapolis: University of Minnesota Press, 1984.

Weatherford, Jack. *Indian Givers: How the Indians of the Americas Transformed the World.* New York: Fawcett Columbine, 1990.

Young Bear, Ray A. *Black Eagle Child: The Facepaint Narratives.* Iowa City: University of Iowa Press, 1992.

Young Bear, Ray A. *The Invisible Musician.* Duluth, MN: Holy Cow! Press, 1990.

Young Bear, Ray A. *Winter of the Salamander: The Keeper of Importance.* San Francisco: Harper and Row, 1980.